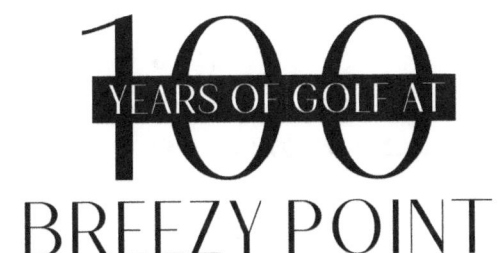

BREEZY POINT

From Walter Hagen to Arnold Palmer

RICH AULIE

GLASS**SPIDER**PUBLISHING

Cover design by Judith S. Design & Creativity
www.judithsdesign.com
Published by Glass Spider Publishing
www.glassspiderpublishing.com

To Dave and Don...

Dave Gravdahl, AKA Mr. Breezy Point, started working at the resort as a caddy back in 1953 and worked his way up the ladder to become general manager of Breezy Point in 1982, a position he held until his death in 2024. Dave was involved in most of the golf expansion at Breezy Point and provided me with boxes of pictures and articles he kept about golf at Breezy Point. This is a book of stories and, with 70 years at the resort, Dave was the master storyteller.

Don Peddie was a Harvard graduate who first played golf at Breezy Point in the 1930s. Don wrote a golf column for the Country Echo in the 1980s and 90s and kept track of everything golf in the area. Thanks to publisher Pete Mohs, I was able to read over 100 of his columns. Together with Dave Gravdahl, their dream was to preserve the history of golf here. They planned to create a small museum-styled display of Breezy Point golf at the Traditional clubhouse. This book is an extension of that dream. I think they would have enjoyed reading it, and I hope you will, too.

Contents

Introduction

On a warm, humid afternoon in the summer of 2018, Slick Rick walked up to the tee box on the par 5 fourth hole at Whitebirch Golf Course in Breezy Point, Minnesota.

Sweat dripping down his back, he bent down and teed up his Titleist Pro V1. He stepped back behind the ball, looked down the fairway toward the green that lay 503 yards away, and aligned himself.

He picked at his sweaty shirt, which was stuck to his torso. He checked his grip. When he was satisfied, he walked up to the ball and took his stance.

As a small gallery watched, he took a calming breath, drew his driver back, and smoked the ball right down the middle.

He glanced up briefly to assure himself that the ball was heading straight. He tossed his driver aside and quickly picked up his golf bag, which held just a 3 wood, wedge, and putter. Then he took off on a dead sprint toward his ball, which lay 280 yards away in the middle of the fairway.

When he reached it, he took another calming breath and smoothed his 3 wood up just short of the green. Racing to the ball, he used his wedge to pitch the ball close to the hole. Then he ran over to the ball and tapped it in for birdie.

He glanced over at the gallery. When he saw the thumbs up, Rick raised his arms in triumph.

The small gallery ran to join in the celebration. Slick Rick had just set the world record for the fastest hole in golf in a time of one minute and 39.2 seconds.

More importantly, Rick had just added his name to the cast of characters who have inhabited the Breezy Point Golf Club over the last hundred years.

Chapter 1: Expect the Unexpected

To expect the unexpected shows
a thoroughly modern intellect.
–Oscar Wilde, *An Ideal Husband*

Oscar Wilde's play about deceit, conspiracy, and bribery among the English upper class has been used as a plot for several movies.

The story also seems to have played out during the Roaring Twenties at Breezy Point. Deceit, conspiracy, bribery, and even murder were all part of the early days at the resort and the people who lived and visited there.

Expect the unexpected.

The Cast of Characters

Wilford H. Fawcett, aka "Captain Billy"
Our Motto: "Make it Snappy" –*Captain Billy's Whiz Bang,* 1919

Following World War I, the Roaring Twenties gave American people time to enjoy life, indulge themselves, and maybe even get rich quick. Captain Wilford H. Fawcett was one of those lucky enough to strike it rich. A veteran of both the Philippine-American War and World War I, Fawcett spent part of his time in the army writing copy for the *Stars and Stripes* newspaper. Returning to civilian life in Robbinsdale, he became a reporter for the *Minneapolis Tribune* covering the "hotel beat." He wrote about celebrity guests and was known on occasion to embellish a story to make for better reading. Soon after that, he opened a speakeasy downtown and was a bootlegger who paid for protection. In 1919, he started publishing a men's humor magazine called *Captain Billy's Whiz Bang*. The risqué cartoon and joke magazine got its name from the sound artillery shells made during the war. The first issue sold 2,000 copies. By 1921, *Captain Billy's Whiz Bang* was selling 350,000 copies a month. It was the start of the Fawcett Publishing empire that would make Billy Fawcett a very wealthy man.

1921 was also the year Fawcett used some of his newfound wealth to purchase an 80-acre tract on Big Pelican Lake in Northern Minnesota called Breezy Point. Breezy Point was a playground for Captain Billy's family and his celebrity friends. His guests would spend summer days going on airplane excursions, viewing Fawcett's native animal zoo, and enjoying the water wheel and water slide on the beach, as well as playing tennis, fishing, horseback riding, bowling, and trap shooting. Captain Fawcett was a crack shot and was the captain of the U.S. trap shooting team that won the gold medal at the 1924 Paris Olympics. An avid big-game hunter, Billy traveled from Alaska to Africa in search of prized trophy heads he would display on the walls of the lodge at Breezy Point.

These were the days of the Roaring Twenties, and roar they did at Breezy Point with Billy Fawcett as the host. Girls in bobbed hairdos and flapper outfits and men in zoot suits danced the Charleston to the music of world-famous orchestras at the Supper

Club as soft lights flickered from sparkling cut-glass chandeliers. If they weren't dancing, guests could be found in Breezy's casino. The resort had a flourishing gambling business during the Fawcett era, thanks in part to his friend Robert Hamilton.

Hamilton knew Captain Billy from the early days in Minneapolis when Fawcett was struggling to make a living. A summer resident on the north shore of Pelican Lake, Bob Hamilton came on board to set up and run a casino featuring two roulette wheels, craps tables, and poker tables. Several slot machines were located throughout the main lodge as well.

Hamilton ran the casino for a number of years until, after a disagreement with Captain Billy, he left to run a casino in the British West Indies for 22 years. Author Sinclair Lewis spent the summer of 1926 at the Hamilton residence on Pelican Lake, writing his novel *Elmer Gantry* during the day and partying at Breezy Point at night.

Sinclair Lewis was not the only celebrity to show his face at Breezy Point. Fawcett was friends with many Hollywood celebrities, sports stars, and politicians of the era. Some could be identified with just a single name: Gable, Lombard, Dempsey, Harlow, and Bing, to name just a few.

When he wasn't running his magazine empire or on a hunting trip, Billy could be found hanging out with the stars in Hollywood. The movie industry was a pretty tight-knit group, but Fawcett would cater to the stars to get the latest gossip for his movie magazines. His contagious personality helped him make many friends in Hollywood. In the summer he was at his resort on Pelican Lake, and the celebrities would go there to hang out with Captain Billy. Not bad for a man who only had an eighth-grade education.

Isadore Blumenfeld, aka "Kid Cann"
"Of course it was an accident—he was always playing Russian roulette." –Kid Cann, 1924

It was the age of Prohibition, but guests at Breezy Point didn't have to go far to enjoy a cocktail or two as the resort had its own speak-easy with illegal liquor smuggled in by plane, train, and automobile. On occasion, an airplane might drop an illegal cache of liquor that would be picked up in the bay in front of the resort. Isadore Blumenfeld was born in Romania in 1900 and moved to Minneapolis with his family when he was two years old. He grew up in a poor Jewish neighborhood in north Minneapolis. Isadore dropped out of school at an early age to work as a paperboy and help out his family. Quickly learning the ways of the streets, he rose fast in the ranks and soon branched out into other not-so-legal moneymaking schemes. It was during this time that he received the nickname "Kid Cann," which would follow him for the rest of his life. Ostensibly, every time there was trouble around, Blumenfeld could be found hiding in the latrine, or "can"!

During Prohibition, Cann ventured into the bootlegging business, bringing whiskey from Canada, rum from Louisianna, and moonshine from Minnesota to customers throughout the Upper Midwest. No doubt Captain Billy would have known Cann from his days running a speakeasy in Minneapolis. If Breezy Point didn't get their illegal liquor from Blumenfeld directly, he certainly would have had a hand somewhere along the line in its distribution.

Another Roaring Twenties get-rich-quick story, Kid Cann was a capo in the Minneapolis Jewish mob known as Murder, Inc., which was run by Meyer Lansky out of New York City. The mob received protection from their illegal activities by bribing Minneapolis and St. Paul policemen and politicians. In April 1924, Cann shot and killed Charles Goldberg after an argument in front of the Vienna Café on Nicollet Avenue in Minneapolis. Cann admitted to the shooting, but he had a legal ally. Having grown up in the same North Minneapolis neighborhood as Cann and many other gangsters, Floyd B. Olson was serving a second term as Hennepin County Attorney. The murder was ruled an accident. Kid Cann did not serve any time in jail.

Floyd B. Olson, AKA "Skipper"
Ten thousand Jews were making booze,
without the state's permission.
To fill the needs of a million Swedes,
who voted for Prohibition.
–Poem by Walter Liggett, found in
Captain Billy's Whiz Bang, November 1926

A Scandinavian kid of modest means, Floyd Bjornstjerne Olson
grew up in the same North Minneapolis neighborhood as Isadore
Blumenfeld and had established a strong connection with the

Jewish community there. Soon after getting his law degree, he began working for Hennepin County (Minneapolis), becoming the county attorney when his boss was fired for accepting bribes in 1920. Floyd had a cabin on Gull Lake near Brainerd and was a frequent guest at Breezy Point in the 1920s

Olson's biographer, George Mayer, recalled one such trip there in 1926. Leaving a day early for a Minnesota State Bar Association meeting in Duluth, Floyd suggested to his friend and traveling partner George Leonard that they make a detour west to Breezy Point.

"When they arrived at the lodge at Breezy, he and Leonard encountered a noisy crowd centering around Sinclair Lewis, then at the height of his fame. Leonard's weak protests failed to dissuade Olson from introducing himself and joining the party. Eventually it moved to Sinclair Lewis' cabin, where Olson exchanged yarns with the novelist for some hours. Lewis was working on Elmer Gantry at the time, and the convivial evening ended with the singing of hymns. They never met again, but Sinclair Lewis remembered Olson well enough to use him for one of the characters in his 1935 novel, It Can't Happen Here. The next morning Floyd remarked that the opening sessions at conventions were always dull and proposed a further detour to another resort he liked, promising his companion the best chicken dinner in Minnesota."

It happened again the following day as Leonard began to realize that Olson had never intended to reach Duluth. They didn't.

According to Mayer, "In Olson, strains of energy and sloth, ambition and carefree gaiety were woven together to create a complex and contradictory personality."

Olson could be mischievous and fun-loving and always enjoyed a good prank, as the following story from the *Brainerd Dispatch* recounts:

Marathon Run From Breezy Point To Pequot

Breezy Point Lodge, Pequot, Minn. July 13, 1927 – Two athletes of prominence trotted a Marathon from Breezy Point
Lodge to Pequot, a hot, grueling five-mile run over graveled
roads, and won their contention that it could be done. The
runners were Floyd Olson, Minneapolis, county attorney of
Hennepin County, who fifteen years ago was a track star at
Hamline and had an idea he could come back; and Herbert
Crummy, Hollywood, Calif. golf professional, who ran for
the West High School, Minneapolis, track team years ago,
grabbing honors. Carl J. Coleman, Minneapolis, organized
the event, betting real money neither runner would finish.
Captain W. H. Fawcett motored along, and fifteen other cars
trailed the runners, who made the grind in fifty minutes. And
then to show he wasn't winded, Olson wheeled Crummy
two miles on the country road, using a squeaky old wheel-
barrow as the vehicle.

Olson was elected governor of the state of Minnesota in 1930
and would serve three terms until his death in 1937. He was a charismatic leader, both charming and energetic. Like Franklin Roosevelt, he used radio broadcasts to stay in touch with the people. He
was considered a progressive politician who could also be more
pragmatic when needed. He did, however, possess his own personal flaws, including a weakness for both alcohol and women.

Antoinette Fawcett, aka the Henna-Haired Hurricane
"Before a man marries, he swears to love. After marriage, he
loves to swear!" –*Whiz Bang Filosophy*, 1921

Billy Fawcett must have liked to swear. Married three times and
twice divorced, he certainly knew his share of marital bliss and
strife. In October of 1929, Captain Billy and his second wife, Antoinette Fisher Fawcett, were preparing to leave New York City for
an African safari.

When interviewed by the *New York American* at the Ritz Carlton,
Mrs. Fawcett resignedly admitted she was going to Africa "to hunt
things."

Her adventurous husband had just returned from British Co-
lumbia with a few dozen caribou, mountain sheep, and other

animals. Mrs. Fawcett said, "I understand you have to wash your hair in benzine in some places in Africa, but I'm game. Billy is away from the family so much I must go with him this time. Besides, I want to check up on his stories of killing grizzlies."

Claire Windsor, a guest of the Fawcetts, smiled and said, "I've been in Africa, my dear, and it simply ruins your nails." Captain Billy snorted in disgust.

The Roaring Twenties was a decade that featured a rapid expansion of the U.S. stock market marked by wild speculation from investors. Stocks of companies were valued way over their actual worth as the market spun out of control. The stock market crash of 1929 occurred on October 24, 1929, a day known as "Black Thursday." It would usher in the worst economic disaster in U.S. history: the Great Depression. The stock market had risen over 20% each year from 1922 to 1929. By 1932, three years after the crash, the stock market had lost 90% of its value from its high point in 1929. Although some people lost all their money, most of the very wealthy Americans were not affected as much by the Depression. Family businesses continued to do well. Hollywood was still very wealthy. Magazines continued to sell as Americans looked for an escape from their troubles in the gossip and stories they could read in *True Confessions, Screen Secrets,* and of course, *Captain Billy's Whiz Bang.* Captain Billy continued to prosper. While Wall Street was crashing on October 24, 1929, Mr. and Mrs. W.H. Fawcett were leaving New York City to go on an African safari.

Twenty-five years old when they married in 1922, Antoinette was Billy Fawcett's Roaring Twenties bride, and she appeared to act the part. Mrs. Fawcett liked the wealth she married into and enjoyed the company of celebrities and important people who were always hanging around her husband. It turned out she may have liked some of them a little more than she should have. Filing for divorce from his wife in 1931, Captain Billy testified that his wife had been vile and indecent and lacked the proper respect and loyalty of a wife. He said she had humiliated him and was ready to name several men as co-respondents in the divorce proceedings, if necessary. Six Breezy Point employees testified on behalf of Mr. Fawcett. It was reported that Mrs. Fawcett had purchased clothes and an automobile for one of her gigolos, who was a golf professional. When his wife did not contest the court proceedings, Captain Billy was granted a divorce in May of 1932.

Antoinette gave this statement to the newspaper: "My friends know that I am innocent of charges brought against me in the suit and they know the men named by Mr. Fawcett in the suit are also innocent. Nothing would have been gained by forcing the suit to trial except my own reputation would have been cleared. I agreed to drop the fight to save the names of innocent men who have been dragged into the suit."

Mrs. Fawcett used the money from her divorce settlement to purchase her own men's magazine, the *Calgary Eye Opener*. She would also turn out to be connected to three men involved in a Minneapolis murder in December of 1935.

With the repeal of Prohibition in 1934, bootleggers like Kid Cann had to look for other means to control the flow of liquor in Minnesota. That control was now in the form of liquor licenses, and the mob sought to obtain a monopoly on them in order to keep the supply of liquor under their control. Governor Olson's hand-picked advisors, known as the "All-Party Machine," helped determine who got a license to sell liquor. Most of the group were heavy drinkers themselves, especially the ones who often vacationed with the governor at Breezy Point Lodge on Pelican Lake. Journalist Walter Liggett published a small newspaper, the *Midwest American*, in which he sought to expose the connection between organized crime and local and state government in the time right after the repeal of Prohibition. Liggett was picking up the torch left by journalist Howard Guilford, who was murdered in 1934 after calling out Governor Olson and his friends for their many ties to organized crime. Liggett was arrested on a morals charge involving two underage girls in 1935. The alleged incident had occurred almost a year and a half earlier and seemed contrived as a means to discredit and silence Walter.

Minneapolis journalist Walter Liggett
"He is a damned sight more of a racketeer than he is a radical."
–Walter Liggett on Governor Floyd Olson

In need of help, Liggett answered a call from Antoinette Faw-cett telling him she had information about his trial that she wanted to discuss with him. On October 24, he went to Mrs. Fawcett's suite at the Radisson Hotel, where she routinely entertained politi-cians, newspapermen, lawyers, and even gangsters. Members of the All-Party Machine were frequent guests there, including one of her former paramours, Governor Floyd Olson. Antoinette had noth-ing new to tell Liggett. The meeting was set up so her friend Kid Cann could have a chance to talk to Walter.

After refusing a bribe from Cann in exchange for stopping his attack on him in the newspaper, the two men began arguing over drinks and nearly came to blows. It was time to leave. Cann offered to give Liggett a ride home, and the two men stopped along the way for one more drink at a local nightclub. Walter was attacked there by seven members of Cann's gang and beaten so badly that he was put in the hospital.

Walter was acquitted in his trial shortly after getting out of the hospital. It would have been a good time to leave town, but Liggett couldn't be bought and wouldn't be scared away. He stepped up his attack in the paper, calling for the impeachment of Governor Olson and listing twelve separate charges against him involving no-torious immorality, favoritism, graft, and fraud. Three days after that story was published, Walter Liggett was the victim of a gang-land drive-by shooting right in front of his apartment, with his wife and daughter sitting in a car witnessing the attack. Five bullets struck his heart and ended his life. Liggett's wife, Edith, identified the gunman as Isadore Blumenfeld, otherwise known as Kid Cann.

Cann was indicted for the murder of Walter Liggett on Decem-ber 21. At the murder trial, Mrs. Liggett identified Cann as the shooter and also stated that "the murder would not have been committed without Governor Olson's permission. He either ordered it or permitted it."

For Cann's part, he had an alibi. According to several witnesses, he was at the barbershop at the time of the murder. From his bed at St. Mary's Hospital in Rochester, Governor Olson also denied any part in the murder, saying, "Mrs. Liggett, in her bereavement, is entitled to and has the sympathy of everyone. But that does not give her the right to make false and unfair statements such as her charge that I was connected with the murder of her husband. I hope it was not inspired by some politician."

Nine days later, despite two eyewitness testimonies that Cann was the shooter, the jury found him not guilty of the murder of Walter Liggett. Six months later, Edith Liggett had moved her family to New York for safety, Governor Olson died after a battle with stomach cancer, and it was business as usual for the crime syndicate and government in Minnesota. Kid Cann kept his hand in the business until he was sent to prison in 1961 for trying to bribe a juror in another case in which he was involved. Antoinette Fawcett was out of the limelight for less than two years. In 1938, the self-proclaimed "Henna-Haired Hurricane" magazine publisher was arrested on five counts of sending obscene matter through the mail. She received a $1,000 fine and was placed on three years' probation. That was the end of her publishing career.

Her ex-husband, Captain Billy, noted in a newspaper column, "There is one campaign that will get my pat on the back and that's the movement to rid our newsstands of the so-called naughty magazines. The movement has already been started. All the better publishers are in favor of it."

It is a note of interest that the original "naughty" magazine, *Captain Billy's Whiz Bang*, was no longer being published. Mrs. Fawcett was arrested for shoplifting shortly afterward. Antoinette was a known kleptomaniac. Captain Billy would arrange for shop owners in Pequot to keep track of items she took from their stores during their time at Breezy Point, and he would always reimburse them for the merchandise she stole. In November of 1939, she failed to appear in court on a probation violation. Antoinette moved to Southern California and eventually remarried.

This was all a part of the backdrop in the early days at Breezy Point, where people ran loose and free. Along with alcohol and gambling, golf became a prime source of entertainment for Breezy Point's guests. In an April 1923 letter to the president of the Brainerd Golf Club, Captain Billy wrote, "Mrs. Fawcett and I took our first lessons in golf at Pinehurst, NC last winter, so that germ has been planted."

Like many wealthy men who had spent time at Pinehurst, Fawcett returned home determined to build a golf course similar to the Donald Ross designs he saw at the resort. He also had the good fortune to have land available at Breezy Point that was very similar to Pinehurst. Playing in a professional golf tournament there in the 1930s, Billy Fawcett's friend Les Bolstad wrote, "This country (Pinehurst) with its sand hills and pines and with the bunch grass for rough resembles nothing so much as Breezy Point."

The land available for Fawcett's golf course had a century earlier been the site of Native American battles between the Chippewa and Sioux nations. Some of the land was now being used as an airstrip for Captain Billy's planes. A wealthy man with only an eighth-grade education who wasn't much of a golfer, Billy Fawcett decided to build a golf course in his backyard. And with that, 100 years of golf at Breezy Point got its start.

Chapter 2: The Roaring Twenties

This black-and-white photo, probably from the early 1930s, shows a wide-open golf course. There are thirty sand traps in the picture, which include the long par-5 third hole, the par-3 fourth hole going down toward the lake, and the par-5 fifth hole (now #8) coming back along the road. Those holes have all been either changed or eliminated.

The original nine-hole golf course at Breezy Point was called Chippewa Links. Some of the holes remain and are part of what is today called the Traditional Golf Course. In September of 1921, we find the first mention of golf at Breezy Point in a *Brainerd Dispatch* article on the resort. The newspaper reported that "near the flying field an 18-hole golf course will be laid out by an expert. No pains will be spared to make it an up-to-date golf course."

Work began on the course in the summer of 1923 after Captain Billy's visit to Pinehurst. On June 3, 1924, the *Brainerd Dispatch* reported, "The nine-hole golf links are being rapidly completed and will be opened with the Ten Thousand Lakes tournament July 4th, covering three days' playing. The Breezy Point golf club is a member of the Minnesota Golf Association. Roscoe Fawcett is the club's president and Miss Ada Anderson is secretary. Some of the most noted golfers of the area will be entered in the tournament. Captain and Mrs. Fawcett have made every effort to provide a golf course which will compare with the best in the east."

Minnesota's Lt. Governor, Louis Collins, hit the tournament's ceremonial first tee shot and played a complete round. He did not record a score. Billy Fawcett's brother, Captain Roscoe Fawcett, was the qualifying medalist with a four-over-par 76, which enabled him to lay first claim to the course record.

Not much is known about the designer of the original nine. Roscoe was a member of the Minnesota Golf Association executive committee and served as president of the Breezy Point course. He was an accomplished golfer and member of the famed Interlachen Country Club, so it would be safe to assume he had some input and influence in the design.

Link Howatt, Breezy Point's first professional, supervised the golf course construction when he arrived in 1924. Link would go on to design and build golf courses in Minnesota and the western United States after leaving Breezy Point. And then there was the man paying the bills. In April of 1923, Captain Billy wrote about taking golf lessons at Pinehurst, North Carolina, over the winter. Pinehurst was home to famed golf architect Donald Ross, who designed many of the courses in the Pinehurst area. He also contributed to the design of Minnesota classics Interlachen, The Minikahda Club, and Northland Country Club, among others. The small push-up greens at Chippewa Links required accurate irons and a really good short game and gave a Donald Ross Pinehurst touch to the course. The Ross touch may have been influenced by Fawcett's trip to Pinehurst or by Roscoe's connection with Interlachen.

The old number one green at Chippewa Links, now number 10 at the Traditional, is one example of the Donald Ross Pinehurst-styled putting surface. This push-up green was designed to repel less-than-perfect shots into collection areas at the bottom of the slopes.

Indian Lore and Legend Continues at Historic and Beautiful Breezy Point Golf Course at Pequot, Minn.

Interesting and Deceptive Links Located on Shores of Big Pelican Lake - Par 72 Has Never Been Equaled- Roscoe Fawcett Holds Record With a 73

By John F. McGovern

One of the younger golf courses of the state which bids fair to grow into one of the most interesting is the Breezy Point course at Pequot, Minn., on the shores of Big Pelican Lake. The course is only four years old but has been nursed to a state of high efficiency.

The course, an adjunct to the famous Breezy Point Lodge, is situated on historic ground, rich in Indian lore and legend. It was here the Sioux and Chippewa tribes, traditional enemies, fought many bloody battles. The ancient aborigine enemies met frequently when on trading and trapping expeditions to fight out feuds which were never settled.

The lake region in this part of the state was a favorite hunting ground of the Chippewas. The Sioux came north to reap some of the rich harvest of pelts, hides, furs, and meat. They expected battles and frequently found them. Many souvenirs of this early Indian warfare have been found in the vicinity of Breezy Point.

The Indian motif has been preserved in the complexion and adjuncts of the place. Some Chippewa Indians act as caddies. The flags which mark the greens are genuine Chippewa spears made by the Indians and painted with brightly colored paints as was done on the festival days.

The course is a nine-hole arrangement with grass greens. It is well trapped with bunkers and so lined with trees that the statuesque pines which look so charming from the tees become real hazards to the player who strays from the straight and narrow. Much of the course was blazed out of the forest. On those holes where the trees were standing, enough of them were left to frame the greens and set off the fairways.

A delightful view may be had of the lake from many fairways and tees. The vista through the trees across the waters of the big lake or across the wide beach and amusement grounds of the lodge is one that will linger long in the mind of the summer vacationist.

The Breezy Point course is one of those deceptive layouts that seems easy but is fraught with trouble. Even the great Walter Hagen, who played over the links several times, failed to make the scores in the north country which he had been turning in consistently on links that were generally supposed to be more difficult.

The total length of the course is over 6,000 yards. Par is 72. Par has not been equaled, a 73 made by Roscoe Fawcett, president of the club, being the best performance turned in thus far. Herb Crummy, professional, is in regular attendance. He is kept busy teaching the visitors from the southland who come north to enjoy the cool Minnesota summers.

The holes are labeled with their Chippewa names. Number one is Bay-shig; number two Niss-Wi; number three Nee-Win, and so on through the eighteen. Efforts have been made to develop some of the Indian caddies to upset the generally accepted theory that Indians are not natural golf players. One or two of the boys are showing more than the average Indian aptitude for the game, but the outlook is not encouraging. More success was had with the red-skinned club-toters matched against some of the golfers when the Indians were allowed to shoot arrows against golf balls. The Indians won most of those matches. The Indians about Breezy Point are better than the average with bow and arrow because of the archery practice held frequently on the beach. The youths acquire the skill which was once the boast of every Indian with the arrow but have no background for golf.

In the pictures above are shown three views of the course. On the left is the short fourth hole, with traps on two sides. On the right is the fifth fairway looking across from the seventh. Below is the seventh green. Roscoe Fawcett, president of the club, is on the left, and Herb Crummy, pro, is on the right.

–From the *Minneapolis Journal*, July 17, 1927, written by John F. McGovern. McGovern covered golf for the newspaper and was a frequent competitor in the early days of the Ten Thousand Lakes Golf Tournament.

Billy Fawcett was always looking to add to or improve on what he had at his resort. The golf course was no exception. In April of 1926, the *Brainerd Dispatch* reported that "a half-million-dollar land development project is being launched at Breezy Point this summer and planning engineers are staking out an additional nine holes."

Things moved slowly. At Roscoe Fawcett's invitation, Interlachen pro Willie Kidd came to Breezy Point in 1927 to help brush up the golf course. Kidd had just finished creating two new holes for the Donald Ross design at Interlachen, and among the changes made, he lengthened the second hole by 100 yards with a new green set back in the woods to make it a 445-yard par four.

After the 1928 Ten Thousand Lakes Tournament, *The Amateur Golfer* offered these comments on the course:

A pleasing feature of the Breezy Point affair was the improved condition of the course. The greens were true, the fairways in good shape, the rough respectable. The course looked easy. It was not so easy. It was highly deceptive. The boys thought they could go out and make a showing that would misrepresent their golfing ability to their advantage. It did not so happen. The fairways were narrower than the forehead of a moron and there were surviving trees standing along the edges of most of the lawns. The pines and the spruce bore some attractive influence on the stray shots. They were always in the way, always being hit, and always in the line to the green. Two new course records were made. Art Tveraa with a 71 lowered the old mark for the sturdier division of the populace. Mrs. Oren Safford shot an 88 in her round against Mrs. Ralph Little to decrease the figures which record the best performance of a woman.
–From *The Amateur Golfer*, September 1928

In July of 1931, the *Dispatch* again reported:
Several acres of timber have been cleared to make room for the new nine holes to be added to the Breezy Point golf course. The new course, laid out mostly around Big Pelican Lake, will be of championship length when completed and will measure 6,400 yards. The extension will run southward into the McIntyre land holdings of Captain W.H. Fawcett. There are plans for a new golf clubhouse to be erected near the present number four green. A new watering system has just been installed for the course with an immense storage tank holding 70,000 gallons of water.

Captain Fawcett standing by his airplane on the land where he would build his golf course in 1924.

The Haig

The term fabulous is reserved for an even more select group. It is greatness grown into legend. It describes the astonishing and the incredible. It exudes color, magnetic personality, and the intangible something that attracts crowds and makes news both on and off the field. It is as much the manner of victory as the triumphs themselves. In golf, men like Ben Hogan, Byron Nelson, Gene Sarazen, and Sammy Snead wear the cloak of greatness. Bobby Jones rates as perhaps the most brilliant of them all. Walter Charles Hagen can be classed as fabulous.

–Harry Moulter, *Famous American Athletes of Today* (1953)

Walter Hagen was golf's greatest showman. He was often referred to as "Sir Walter" or "The Haig." His legacy as the most colorful character the game has ever seen often overshadows what a great player he was. Jack Nicklaus holds golf's Holy Grail with eighteen major championships in his illustrious career. Tiger Woods, still chasing Jack, currently sits in second place with fifteen majors. Hagen is third on the list with eleven majors, a number made more astonishing when you consider the Masters was not around during the prime of his career. The "fourth major" during Hagen's career was the Western Open, a tournament Sir Walter won five times. Those wins would bring his major total up to sixteen, good for second place behind Nicklaus. Whether you consider him second or third on the list, Hagen's name should be right next to the other two whenever the conversation comes up about the greatest golfer of all time.

Hagen started his golf career as a caddie at the Rochester Country Club (CC) when he was eight years old. At the age of fifteen, he was promoted to assistant pro, and at the age of nineteen was asked to take on the position of head pro at the country club. One year later, he was teeing it up in the U.S. Open in Brookline, Massachusetts. That was the year that American amateur Francis Ouimet defeated the British stars Harry Vardon and Ted Ray in a three-man playoff.

In his first appearance on golf's major stage, Walter Hagen finished fourth, three strokes behind the leaders. He told everyone he was coming back the next year to win the tournament, and true to his word, he went to Midlothian CC in Chicago the next year and won his first U.S. Open. It was the beginning of a run that over the next fifteen years would see Hagen collect one more U.S. Open along with four British Open and five PGA championships. It should be noted that he won the PGA four years in a row from

1924 to 1927. That mark might never be matched.

The Haig is generally considered the greatest match player of all time. With a long game made erratic by a pronounced sway in his swing, he often had to scramble and putt to make his way around the course. Hagen lived by the principle that "three of those and one of them still count four."

Walter felt that only a relaxed golfer could play his best in tournaments. "I decided then that mental and physical relaxation during competition was the most valuable asset any golfer could possess," he said. "Concentrate on playing the best you can on each shot…if it's a good one, that's fine. If it's bad, forget it. I expected to make so many bad ones anyway. I had to recognize that fact and aim to get the good ones where they counted most."

Scottish golf professional Tommy Armour once said of him, "Hagen could relax sitting on a hot stove."

Gene Sarazen commented, "I think Walter Hagen contributed more to golf than any player, today or ever. He took the game all over the world. He popularized it here and everywhere. Walter was at the head of the class; he made professional golf what it is."

Hagen played over 2,000 one-day exhibition matches across the country and around the world in an effort to bring golf to the people. Ultimately, this was his legacy.

Charles Price, in his book *Golfer At Large*, described it best:

Hagen made countless one-day stands in the outlands of America playing matches against all comers, charging spectators a dollar a head and making in the process more money than Babe Ruth- and eventually spending more than the entire Yankee outfield. His exhibitions were a combination of matinee comedy and golfing fireworks.

Al Barkow called it "sprinkling seeds" and referred to the Haig as the "Johnny Appleseed of American Golf."

Walter literally sprinkled seeds during his 1922 exhibition tour in the form of the newly created wooden tee. Before 1920, golfers would pinch sand together to produce a tee for their ball to sit on when teeing off.

In 1920, Dr. William Lowell began whittling wooden tees that could be carried with the golfer and used when teeing off. He painted the tees red and called them the "Reddy Tee."

He paid Hagen and partner Joe Kirkwood $2,500 to use the tees during their exhibition tours. The golfers left a few on every hole for the spectators to pick up and try on their own.

Today, every golfer carries a supply of tees in their golf bag when they go out to play.

I remember Little Falls golf coach Rich Weigel using a thick, stubby tee he referred to as his "carrot tee" because of its shape. His playing partners had to help him look for it if it flew off the tee box, as he proudly used that same tee for several years without breaking it.

Hagen would probably love today's colorful "Martini Tees." Like a Rich Weigel carrot tee, you can use one over and over...unless you lose it.

1925 brought the Hagen exhibition tour to one of his favorite states, Minnesota. On July 17, Sir Walter played the Chippewa Links course at Breezy Point with resort owner Billy Fawcett on hand to direct the proceedings. Hagen played against the new pro, Fred Barber, and defeated him 2 & 1. In a team competition, the Haig played with Father Walter Remmis of Brainerd against Barber and Minneapolis grain merchant Ralph Little. Hagen and Father Remmis won 5 & 3, with the Brainerd priest making the group's first birdie of the day on hole 11.

1920s golfers standing by the first tee. Note the sandbox on the left used for making tees.

The *Brainerd Dispatch* reported: Father Remmis was universally commended for his splendid playing. In spite of the large gallery and the strange field with its hazards, he maintained his poise and powerful stroke. The exhibition tours of famous golfers, such as Hagen is making this year, are of educational value to all amateur golfers. "You have a wonderful course at Breezy Point," said Mr. Hagen, "and the summer resort is as attractive as French Lick in the variety of amusement and recreation offered. I was certainly most agreeably surprised to find such a beautiful resort and appreciate the remarkable hospitality shown by Captain and Mrs. W.H. Fawcett. I am also pleased to see the hold golfing has here and at Brainerd as exemplified by the large gallery at the play."

During this exhibition tour, Sir Walter set course records at four different layouts in Canada and North Dakota. But there would be no course record shot at Breezy Point. Final scores for the four-some on the par-72 course were: Hagen 77, Father Remmis 82, Fred Barber 82, and Ralph Little 84. In a trapshooting contest held after the golf, Captain Billy Fawcett broke 23 out of 25 targets, while Sir Walter broke 18 out of 25.

Never one to miss a good party, Sir Walter rated New Orleans and Minneapolis as two of his favorite cities to visit. He went on to state "for the record" that the Norwegian, Swedish, and Danish girls in Minnesota were among the most attractive he had ever met! In addition, trips to Minnesota usually involved a hunting or fishing trip up north. The Haig always played in the St. Paul Open at Keller Golf Club (GC), and in 1939, he returned to Breezy Point for another exhibition match with his friend, John Montague.

Billy Fawcett welcomes the crowd gathered around the first tee as Walter Hagen, on the far right, takes some practice swings before teeing off in his 1925 exhibition match at Breezy Point. (from the collections of the Minnesota Historical Society.)

Captain Roscoe Fawcett

1929 Ten Thousand Lakes finalists Harry Howe and Roscoe Fawcett. Always the bridesmaid, Fawcett would defeat Howe 4 & 3 to finally win the championship.

Les Bolstad remembered Roscoe Fawcett as a good player with a big mustache. Roscoe started out as a sports editor for a Portland, Oregon newspaper covering football, baseball, golf, and tennis. An airplane gunner during World War I, Captain Fawcett survived a plane crash in England during the war, with the main damage done to his upper lip; hence, the mustache he sported to cover it up.

In 1922, when his brother needed help managing the resort at Breezy Point, Roscoe moved back to Minnesota to become a vice president of Fawcett Publishing and also received a 25% share in the resort. Captain Billy looked to his brother for golf planning, marketing, and financial advice. Roscoe also had contacts with many of the Hollywood celebrities who came to Breezy in the early days. He was a close friend of Jean Harlow, the Marilyn Monroe of her day. Roscoe had considerable input into the Ten Thousand Lakes Tournament, as well. A member of Interlachen Country Club, he was able to use that connection to get many of the state's best players to come to Breezy Point and play in the tournament. It was his idea to create a separate division for women, which was mostly unheard of in those days. Ten Thousand Lakes champion Stan Larson recalled Roscoe being a flamboyant, debonair presence on the golf course.

Captain Fawcett had a solid, all-around game. He was extremely competitive and loved a good prank. Roscoe is credited with making the first hole in one in the Lakes area when he sank his tee shot on the 136-yard fourth hole at Breezy Point's Chippewa Links course in August of 1925. Fawcett also tied the course record at Chippewa Links when he shot a 1-under-par 71 there in 1927. He won the Birchmont and Resorters championships in 1927 and, after two runner-up finishes at Breezy, finally took home the Ten Thousand Lakes title in 1929 with a 4 & 3 victory over Harry Howe of Minneapolis. Only two golfers, Maurice Cain and Kenny Pinns, have won the Ten Thousand Lakes title as well as the other three Minnesota resort tournaments: the Birchmont, Resorters, and Pine to Palm. Pinns won all four in the same year! Three golfers have won the Ten Thousand Lakes title and two of the other three: Harry Legg, Bev Vanstrom, and Roscoe Fawcett. Legg and Vanstrom are both members of the Minnesota Golf Hall of Fame. Pretty heady company. Well played, Roscoe!

Richard Coyle Lilly – Banker and Philanthropist

R.C. Lilly, 1924 Ten Thousand Lakes champion

A restless, creative, charismatic Irishman with a keen sense of humor, R.C. Lilly was a tough competitor who played to win. When his father became injured at work, Lilly was forced to drop out of school at the age of fifteen to help support his family. He began his career as a messenger at Merchants National Bank when he was sixteen. Through persistence, dedication, and skill, he steadily moved up the ladder at the bank. Returning to school, he took night classes and eventually received a law degree. He was named an assistant cashier when he was 27 years old. Shortly after that, a bank merger resulted in his promotion to vice president of the bank. Lilly's creative imagination and gift for making quick decisions led to a final promotion to president of what would later become the First National Bank of St. Paul at the age of 33.

Richard Lilly's leadership as a banker was tied to his efforts to find places to invest his bank's money. Tri-State Telephone was purchased by the bank with an eye toward future growth in the communication industry. It was combined with other smaller companies to form what is now U.S. West Communications (Qwest). A small air-service company in Michigan specializing in mail delivery was purchased and moved to Minnesota. It became Northwest Airlines, with Lilly serving as its president for many years. Log Cabin syrup was bought, developed, and sold some years later to General Foods. A small manufacturer of lawn equipment Lilly chose to invest in became the Toro Company, with Lilly's son David serving as president. After World War II, Lilly invested in a company started by some young engineers who had been working for the Navy during the war. It was called Engineering Research Associates. ERA eventually became Control Data. When it came to business, Richard Lilly had the Midas touch!

An accomplished golfer, R.C. Lilly was a charter member at Somerset Country Club in St. Paul. He won the inaugural Ten Thousand Lakes Tournament at Breezy Point in 1924, defeating local favorite Roscoe Fawcett in the finals, 3 & 2. He also won two Minnesota Senior Amateur championships in 1936 and 1943. His reputation as a tough competitor served him well in those match-play competitions, and his game held up well through the years.

Mr. Lilly was known as a hard-drinking, hard-driving, hard-headed businessman who was ambitious and highly competitive. On March 20, 1938, he played 18 holes of golf at Somerset and stopped for a few drinks with friends on the way home. Lilly dozed off behind the wheel of his Chrysler Airflow and drove off the east end of the High Bridge on his way to Mendota Heights. Rescuers had to pry his body out of the upside-down car. The all-steel body of his vehicle probably saved his life, but he required months of surgery followed by a long period of recuperation. Given time to reflect, and guided by his strong Irish-Catholic faith, Richard C. Lilly decided to spend the rest of his life in thanksgiving to God. He was 53 years old.

In 1944, Lilly began work on the Coyle Foundation, which over the next fifteen years donated over $500,000 for charitable, civic, and educational purposes. Through the years, Richard contributed an additional $500,000 of his own money to keep the foundation going. He was known to search the papers for stories about people in need. A poor family may have lost their home in a fire, only to find the house rebuilt through an anonymous donor. A burned child received plastic surgery, or an impoverished high school student suddenly had tuition for college. Often, no one knew where the help came from.

Sister Anna Marie Meyer had been in an automobile accident herself. Her back was broken, causing her to be confined to a wheelchair for the rest of her life. The nun began teaching students with speech and learning problems due to cerebral palsy. After watching the gift she had for reaching these students, Lilly told her, "I'm going to give you a school." The Christ Child School for Exceptional Children is now part of the University of St. Thomas and is used to train today's special education teachers.

Archbishop Murray of St. Paul asked Mr. Lilly for assistance in finding a way to help alcoholic priests. Soon after, land was purchased for the site which would become the Hazelden Foundation in Center City, Minnesota. Lilly was a longtime supporter of the Little Sisters of the Poor and helped raise $400,000 for remodeling of their site in St. Paul's Irving Park. Late in life, Richard Lilly was the campaign chairman charged with raising four million dollars to build the six-floor, 150-bed Divine Redeemer's Hospital in St. Paul. He did not live to see the project, though. Today, it is Health East's Bethesda Care Center.

Richard C. Lilly loved to play golf and was a businessman extraordinaire. He packed enough into his life to last three lifetimes. The success he achieved allowed him to give back a considerable amount of what he had been given and be a blessing to so many other people. It was a life well lived!

*Virginia Brainard Kunz's article on R.C. Lilly in the Ramsey County History (fall of 1998) provided valuable research and information on this remarkable man's life.

Harry George Legg (1886-1930)

When Harry Legg was a youngster, he bought his first golf club from a caddie for 15 cents. The first time he swung it, the clubhead flew farther than the ball and was never found. Legg then bought two better clubs for 89 cents and was on his way to becoming a self-made golfer. Harry won his first big tournament, the National Interscholastic, in 1907 while attending Lawrenceville Prep School in New Jersey. He went on to graduate from Yale University, where he excelled in both basketball and golf. While at Yale, he was ranked as one of the top ten amateur golfers in the country.

A steady player, Harry was a determined, courageous, and canny competitor who played at his best when under pressure. Legg won ten Minnesota State Amateur championships in a 15-year period between 1905 and 1920, a record which has stood for over 100 years.

On the national front, Harry won five Trans-Mississippi championships from 1907-1919 and took the Western Amateur in 1919, defeating Richard Bockenkamp 2-up in the finals.

In 1925, Legg became the first amateur to win the State Open when he shot a four-round total of 297 at Interlachen CC to defeat the state's top professional and amateur golfers.

Harry's short game was legendary. He once played the first five holes at The Minikahda Club and only used three putts! After winning the Western Amateur in 1919, the members at Minikahda awarded Legg an honorary lifetime membership. Harry came out of retirement in 1926 to compete in the U.S. Amateur at his home course. Well past his prime, the portly and bespectacled Legg faced defending champion George Von Elm in the second round. Two-down at the turn, he used his home-course knowledge to win the first four holes on the back nine and held on to win the match 1-up. Harry was two-under-par for the final nine holes. That tough match took its toll on him as an exhausted Legg lost a close-fought quarterfinal match to Walker Cup star Roland MacKenzie 1-up. Bobby Jones defeated Chick Evans 8 & 7 in the finals to win his third Amateur championship at The Minikahda Club.

Harry competed in the Ten Thousand Lakes Tournament from 1926 to 1929. His semifinal match in 1926 featured two of the state's best players going head-to-head when Legg took on 18-year-old Les Bolstad. Bolstad ended Harry's run in the tournament with a 3 & 2 decision. The year 1927 gave golf fans at Breezy Point a rematch as the two golfers hooked up in the semifinals again. Legg prevailed this time with a keenly contested 1-up victory. Harry made four birdies in the finals against veteran Dave Tallman to win their match and the championship 6 & 4. Legg swept all the honors in 1928, winning the qualifying medal with a 75 and defeating 1926 champion Art Tveraa 2 & 1 in the finals to claim his second straight Ten Thousand Lakes cup. In a match followed by more than a hundred people, Harry was 1-under-par for the day. He needed to play that well as Tveraa was only 1-over-par for the match. In addition to his two Ten Thousand Lakes championships, Legg also held two Resorters crowns and one Birchmont title.

Harry Legg sits with his many golf trophies, including two Ten Thousand Lakes cups. His 1928 Ten Thousand Lakes medalist cup is on display at the Breezy Point Traditional Clubhouse.

After winning at Breezy Point in 1928, he declared that 1929 would be his comeback year. If his health held up, something he hadn't been able to enjoy for a while, Harry would enter more tournaments, including the state amateur, the next year. Unfortunately, his health did not improve. He returned to Breezy Point to try for a third title in a row but lost out in the first round. With his kidneys failing, he went in for an operation in January of 1930 but did not survive. Harry Legg, the most successful amateur in Minnesota golf history, died at the age of 43.

The House on Hardwood Point

Other than Captain Billy Fawcett's home at Breezy Point, the largest lodge-style house on Pelican Lake is on Hardwood Point, known today as Weaver's Point. The home dates from the "Roaring Twenties" and has a storied history connected to the Ten Thousand Lakes Golf Tournament.

Ralph and Minerva "Minnie" Little were friends of Billy Fawcett. Ralph was president of the Rex Grain Company in Minneapolis. When Fawcett opened his golf course with the Ten Thousand Lakes Golf Tournament in 1924, Mrs. Little won the women's title. She would go on to win five more times: in 1925, 1926, 1929, 1930, and 1932. Minnie also won the Minnesota Women's Amateur in 1926.

Minerva "Minnie" Little, a six-time
Ten Thousand Lakes Women's Champion

Ralph Little was also a good player. A member of Minneapolis Golf Club, he was a regular at the Ten Thousand Lakes Tournament, often competing in the championship flight. Ralph played with Walter Hagen when he came to Breezy Point for his exhibition match in 1925, shooting an 84 to Hagen's 77.

Captain Billy used the architecture firm Magney and Tusler to design his lodge in 1924 and the Fawcett house in 1926. The 70-foot-long Norway pine logs used for those projects came from the Bemidji area. The Littles bought the property of land on Hardwood Point from Captain Fawcett and his second wife, Antoinette. It's not known whether the log house on the property was built by the Littles or earlier by Fawcett. What is known is that there are several features the Little and Fawcett houses have in common. It would suggest they shared the same architect and source of logs to create the two Swiss chalet lodge-style houses with massive stone fireplaces. The two-story, 4,109-square-foot lodge house overlooks 330 feet of sugar sand beach, surrounded by 20 acres of meadowland. It was used as a summer lake home to entertain the Littles' many friends; they had no children.

In 1935, Ralph Little was killed in an auto accident just north of Nisswa. After scraping the side of his car against a guardrail, Ralph got out to inspect the damage. As he stood outside, the car began to roll backward across the road. An oncoming vehicle was unable to stop, and Mr. Little was crushed between the two cars. He did not survive. Mrs. Little became hysterical and was taken to the Brainerd hospital for treatment before returning home. Minnie would later remarry, and she bought another house on Gull Lake. The Pelican Lake house sat empty for several years until Art and Harriet Weaver purchased it from Mrs. Little in 1959. The Weavers had four boys and named their log home Tau-Pa-Ne-Sim, a Native American name meaning "four brothers."

There was a rumor that the Littles' house was connected to Breezy Point during the 1920s and 30s. Supposedly, the home was rented to Fawcett for use as an illicit gambling site, although no records were ever found to support that claim. After buying the house, the Weavers discovered a trap door leading to a basement. In the basement, they discovered 43 slot machines with money still in them! No one seems to know why all the slot machines were there. Perhaps this was a place where Breezy Point guests came to party and gamble, hidden from the searching eyes of the law. Art Weaver Jr. remembers his youngest brother taking the coins to Pequot Lakes and buying candy. Art told me he wishes they would have hung onto some of those valuable coins from the 1920s!

James Henderson, in his article "Vintage Cabins and Cottages on Pelican Lake," quotes current owners Jeff and Mary Smith on the Ralph Little house: "A place as special as this requires constant upkeep, thoughtful care, and a good sense of humor. We're convinced there is no warmer room than our great room on a cold snowy night with that massive, one-of-a-kind fireplace roaring. We hope to continue to be good stewards in preserving one of the very special places in Northern Minnesota for a long time to come."

Chapter 3: The Great Depression

The 1930s brought several changes in golf equipment. In the 1920s, golfers at Breezy Point might carry seven or eight hickory-shafted clubs with names like driver, brassy, cleek, mashie, iron, niblick, and putter in a small canvas bag. With the huge growth in golf since the middle of the 1920s, perfect pieces of hickory became hard to come by and eventually were replaced by steel shafts. Each hickory shaft would have its own unique quality, while the steel shafts were so uniform that each club had the same feel when the golfer swung it. Spaulding introduced their Robert T. Jones irons in 1930 with steel shafts painted brown to look like the hickory shafts. The lighter-weight steel shafts had a lower balance than hickory, and the ball went farther. By the late 1930s, 95% of all golfers were using steel shafts in their golf clubs.

And then there was the golf ball. The wound-core ball, invented by Coburn Haskell in 1898, would become the standard for the modern golf ball. The Haskell golf ball had a solid core with a layer of rubber thread wrapped around it, covered by a thin outer shell of balata sap. It replaced the gutta-percha ball, giving golfers more distance and lower scores, leading to a surge in golf's popularity. It didn't take long for golf's ruling bodies to react to this new ball. In 1921, the United States Golf Association (USGA) issued this revision to the Rules of Golf: "The Rules of Golf Committee will take whatever steps it thinks necessary to limit the power of the ball with regard to distance."

Competitors in the early days of the Ten Thousand Lakes Tournament played with hickory-shafted golf clubs, teed their ball up on a mound of sand, and used a smaller golf ball. 1931 saw the USGA introduce a new golf ball. Larger and lighter, the new ball would sit up in the grass and be easier to hit, but it wouldn't fly as far as the smaller ball. The new ball was 1.68 inches in diameter and 1.55 ounces in weight as opposed to the old ball, which measured 1.62 inches in diameter and weighed 1.62 ounces. The smaller ball flew straighter, was more wind resistant, and rolled out more than the new larger ball. It was also much easier to control when putting. With the loss in distance, average golfers were in open revolt against the new golf ball and referred to it as the "Balloon Ball."

Breezy Point joined the revolt on July 4, 1931, when, in the spirit of Independence Day, it staged an "Old Ball" tournament at Chippewa Links. The *Brainerd Dispatch* reported on July 1, 1931: "Faulty putting and short drives can no longer be attributed to the much abused 'Balloon Ball' of the United States Golf Association. At least not in the case of the Minnesota golfers who will participate in the July 4th handicap meet at Breezy Point Lodge. Unlike many other tournaments which have all given the entrants the option of either ball, this Independence meet will require all contestants to play with the smaller size golf ball which was last fall outlawed by the governing heads of the golfing world. The new ball, which has so generally displeased the golfers of America, will be banned from the meet. The Breezy Point "old ball" tournament will be an eighteen-hole affair open to both men and women." Thomas Pease of Interlachen shot a low net of 69, and Carl Bettcher of Red Wing won low gross with a score of 83. Governor Floyd Olson won the long drive contest, hitting the smaller golf ball 310 yards!

By September of 1931, it seemed the new ball was a failure in the eyes of many. The USGA was forced to look at making some changes. Most golfers' complaints centered on the lighter weight of the new ball, which made it harder to control, especially when putting. The USGA increased the weight of the new ball to 1.62 ounces and kept the diameter at 1.68 inches effective in 1932. That is the ball we all play today. The Royal and Ancient Golf Association would eventually switch over to the new ball in 1990.

One hundred years after the USGA revision to the Rules of

Golf, there are 90 golfers on the PGA Tour averaging 300 yards or more with their driver. Jack Nicklaus has advocated rolling back the distance on the golf ball for almost 40 years. Augusta National played at 6,985 yards when Nicklaus won the Masters Tournament in 1975. By 2022, the course's yardage had increased to 7,510 yards, with more additions planned for the future. Unfortunately, not every golf course has the room or the money to keep up with the golfers' gains in distance. Golf's governing bodies have recently proposed changes to reduce the distance of the current golf ball and keep golf courses relevant. Hopefully, the changes will go over better than when they first tried changing the ball in 1931.

The number of golf courses in the U.S. reached a peak in 1930 before a steady decline over the next 20 years closed down almost 1,000 courses. Nearly 50 golf courses in Minnesota were put out to pasture—so to speak—during that time. New golf course development came to a halt during the Great Depression, and Breezy Point's second nine holes were never built. In spite of the Depression, Billy Fawcett was financially secure, and the resort carried on with a much smaller clientele. Some weeks, the number of guests was outnumbered four to one by the workers who looked after them. While bread lines in Minneapolis stretched for blocks, Breezy Point guests were eating their meals off of $75 plates with gold inlaid borders. Even though plans for a new nine had been canceled, Breezy Point was able to carry out an improvement program on the existing nine throughout the 1930s.

Archie Houle took over as golf professional at Breezy Point in 1932. Houle got his start in golf as an assistant to Tom Vardon at the White Bear Yacht Club, so he was well acquainted with the Donald Ross style of golf course design. Vardon, his mentor, was also a golf course designer and designed several courses in central Minnesota. Archie himself is credited with designing a nine-hole course for St. John's University in 1926. Under Houle's direction, the Breezy Point course was kept in excellent shape throughout the 1932 season.

New clubhouse built in 1935

In 1935, the *Minneapolis Star* reported, "The Breezy Point golf club has undergone a complete 'face lifting' since last year's event. The first hole has been increased by 30 yards. The third hole has been made over completely, with a new and longer fairway and a new green. Players who would slice their drive used to find their ball in the gully that now is the regular fairway. The new hole will also eliminate players from hooking their second shot into players teeing off on the first hole. The seventh likewise has undergone changes and is 30 yards longer. Expansive, well-sodded tees have been built for each hole with extensive landscaping done. In addition, a new clubhouse has been built off the first tee. The course features a 6,360-yard layout with over 30 tricky bunkers, exceedingly fast greens, and treacherous rough."

The new fairway and green for hole three

The golf course was completely re-seeded and top-dressed in 1936. The next year saw the start of a three-year construction and improvement program for the Breezy Point Golf Club. Under the direction of Captain Fawcett's friend and course manager, Otis Dypwick, all the traps were cleaned up and refurbished, over 200 young pine trees were planted, three new fairways and two interesting new greens were created, and a comprehensive fairway sprinkling system was installed, with outlets every 50 feet to ensure soft, green fairways.

Otis Dypwick

Otis Dypwick served as the golf course manager and tournament director at Breezy Point in the late 1930s. He also played in the Ten Thousand Lakes Tournament from time to time. Otis went to school with golfer Patty Berg and was a lifelong friend of both Patty and Oklahoma football coach Bud Wilkinson. He was a sportswriter for the *Minneapolis Star* during the 1930s and served as the sports information director at the University of Minnesota from 1945 to 1976. Otis co-authored golf instruction books with several professional golfers including Patty Berg and Arnold Palmer. Dypwick's writing style is recognized for its simplistic clarity as well as the fine photography that captured many of the great golf swings of pros from the 40s, 50s, and 60s. His best-selling book, *Winning Golf*, was a collaboration with Byron Nelson. Sales from that book enabled Nelson to retire from tournament golf and buy a ranch in Texas. Otis was hired by Minnesota-based Munsingwear in the late 1950s. He worked with golf professionals to get Munsingwear clothing into golf shops and on the PGA Tour. Anyone who walked into the Breezy Point pro shop in the 1960s and 70s will remember the sight and smell of the distinctive penguin-logoed shirts and sweaters on display. It was the best-selling golf shirt of that era. During his time at Breezy Point, Otis helped Billy Fawcett with the remodeling of the old golf course in the 1930s. In the 1960s, Dypwick collaborated with Totton Heffelfinger in the workup of Hazeltine National Golf Club, the site of several U.S. Opens, two PGA Championships, and a Ryder Cup. He received a lifetime membership at that iconic golf club, #39 on the membership list! Otis Dypwick was inducted into the Minnesota Golf Hall of Fame in 2020, joining his lifelong friend Patty Berg. Deacon's Lodge PGA professional and family friend Mark Neva nominated Otis for the Hall of Fame award.

Les Bolstad, four-time Ten Thousand Lakes Champion: 1925, 1930, 1932, and 1933 (from the collections of the Minnesota Historical Society)

Minnesota's Les Bolstad was a major part of the golf scene at Breezy Point in the 20s and 30s. In 1925, the 17-year-old Bolstad arrived at Breezy Point with eight hickory-shafted golf clubs in a small canvas bag, ready to compete in the second playing of the Ten Thousand Lakes Tournament. He would go on to defeat local favorite Roscoe Fawcett in the finals, 4 & 3. Bolstad would win the Ten Thousand Lakes Tournament three more times, in 1930, '32, and '33 using steel-shafted clubs and the new golf ball the last two years.

Les Bolstad's golf career began as a caddie at the private courses in the Twin Cities. When he wasn't caddying, Les could be found playing and practicing at the city's public golf courses. He won the first State Junior Championship in 1924 at the age of 16. Bolstad captured the State Public Links titles in 1925 and 1926 and went on to win the National Public Links championship in 1926 as well. Les was Minnesota's first national champion in golf.

He would go on to win the State Amateur in 1931 and the State Open in 1933 while he was still an amateur. After turning professional in 1934, Les went on to win the State Open again, in 1938, 1939, and 1943. He also took top honors at the State PGA in 1938, and again in 1951. By 1939, Bolstad had completed a sweep of the state's majors. He is the only golfer in state history to win the Career Grand Slam: the Amateur, Open, PGA, and Public Links.

Les was the Ten Thousand Lakes medalist in 1930 with a two-under-par 70. His finals match with veteran Jake Weatherby was even after nine holes before Bolstad won three of the next four holes with a 2-under-par stretch on his way to winning his second title 3 & 2. Medalist again in 1932 with a 3-under-par 69, Les defeated his younger brother Edgar in the semifinals 4 & 3 only to face another brother, Conway, in the finals. Les was able to claim the Ten Thousand Lakes title as well as the Bolstad family title with a 4 & 2 victory over Conway in their 36-hole final match. In 1933, Les was the Ten Thousand Lakes medalist for the third year in a row with an even par 72. After defeating veteran Dave Tallman in the semifinals, Bolstad would take on Texas newcomer John Barnum in the finals. It would be one of the best matches ever seen at Breezy.

"Big John" Barnum, from Edinburg, TX, was a first-time entrant in the 1933 Ten Thousand Lakes Golf Tournament. Unheralded before coming to Breezy Point, Barnum stepped out of Dave Tallman's automobile on Friday and, despite a stiff wind, shot a 74 on his first trip around the par-72 course. Although he now called Texas home, he was born in Willmar, MN, and went to high school in Minneapolis, hence his connection to the MGA president, also from Willmar. Knowing that Tally liked to bet a few dollars when golfing, there is no doubt he held a stake in Barnum at the pre-tournament Calcutta and probably a few side bets on the newcomer as well.

Ben Gillman gave John a good fight in the first round Saturday, but Gillman had to surrender on the last hole. No one was taking John too seriously yet. Then he took state open champion Lee Herron (grandfather of PGA Tour player Tim Herron) down to the wire. After Herron won the 17th and 18th holes to even the match, Barnum won their semifinal duel with a par on the first extra hole. By now, the gallery realized that Barnum not only drove the ball a long way, but he was also a solid iron player and a wonderful putter.

The long-hitting Texan's final match with defending champion Les Bolstad came down to the last putt on the 18th green. The lead changed hands several times over 18 holes with both golfers playing par golf before an appreciative gallery. Barnum came from two down to square the match on the 17th hole. On the tricky last green,

Big John stroked his birdie try past the hole and three-putted after Bolstad had played his approach putt dead for a par and a 1-up victory.

Barnum turned professional in 1947 and went on to become the head golf professional at Blythfield CC in Grand Rapids, MI. He won the Michigan Open four times in 1950, '58, '60, and '62. He was also a three-time Michigan PGA winner and won the Michigan Senior title five times. When his course was closed during the winter months in the '50s and '60s, he competed on the PGA Tour. John played in 179 PGA Tour events in his career and made the cut 167 times. In 1962, he became the first player to win his first PGA Tour event after turning 50. He is one of only eight golfers to have won on tour after turning 50, joining a list that includes Sam Snead, Phil Mickelson, Davis Love III, and Craig Stadler. Big John, six-foot-three and 220 pounds, shot 18 under par for 72 holes to defeat Gay Brewer by four shots in the 1962 Cajun Classic at Lafayette, LA. Third-place finisher, Bo Wininger, quipped that everyone was pulling for John because "it means some of the rest of us have a lot of golf mileage left in us." The first-place check was worth $2,400. Defending champion Doug Sanders shot even par to finish 30th. He received a check for $20. By comparison, a winner on the PGA Tour today receives a $1,000,000 check, while 30th place pays around $65,000! Barnum would also win the PGA's 1963 Jamaica Open.

His victory was also the first by a player using one of the new PING putters, which were designed and built by Karsten Solheim. Working out of his garage in 1959, Solheim created the model-1A putter featuring weight that kept balance throughout the head of the club. The putter made a distinctive *ping* sound when striking the ball, which led to the company's unique name. Barnum used a newer version at the Cajun Classic, the model-69 putter, also known as the "Hot Dog" putter because of its shape.

Perhaps the most valuable collection of putters in the world is the PING Gold Putter Vault. There are almost 3,000 putters in this collection, commemorating winners on the professional tours who used a PING putter. Two gold-plated replicas of the winning putter are created with the winner's name and the name of the tournament they won engraved on the putter. One putter is given to the winner, and the other putter is kept at PING headquarters in Phoenix. The original Barnum used to win the Louisiana tournament was put in the Michigan Golf Hall of Fame when he became a member in 1984.

Les Bolstad was an employee at Breezy Point in the early 1930s, available to play golf with any of Captain Billy's guests if asked. Playing with a group of out-of-state guests in July of 1932, Les set a nine-hole record of 31 with six straight birdies and nine one-putt greens! But the best story is the lesson Bolstad got from a Breezy bellhop the next month, recounted in this *Minneapolis Star Tribune* account:

> Breezy Point, Minn., Aug. 13. Bob Derrick of Minneapolis, who is a bell hop here and who will return to the University of Minnesota in the fall, wanted Lester Bolstad to show him how he manages to win so many golf titles. Pretty soon it looked like Bob was showing Lester a few wrinkles. On the first 328-yard par-four hole, Derrick sent the ball to within 100 feet of the green with the first stroke. Then bingo, the ball went in for an eagle.

> "Oh, that's only luck," Bob modestly told his playing partner. I'll never even come close again." But on the next par-four hole, Bob sank a birdie. Lester was skeptical but he

continued playing, explaining his shots. The two played 18 holes but Derrick showed Lester three more birdies besides the eagle on the first. "C'mon and show me how to play, will yuh," Lester now says to Bob.

Captain Billy would later finance Bolstad in his first venture into professional golf. In 1933, he went to Hollywood with Fawcett during the winter to work on his golf game. A picture of Les and movie star Alice Dahl, taken at the Hollywood premiere of *King Kong* at Grauman's Chinese Theater, shows it was not all work and no play for the Minnesota golfer! Fawcett would file this report on Bolstad's golf game in *Captain Billy's Whiz Bang*:

FORE!

Quite a man they have out in Portland, Oregon. He is Dr. O. F. Willing, several times member of American golf teams in international play and finalist in the National Amateur. His chief claim to fame came in Pebble Beach, CA, a few years back when he was in the finals of the National Amateur golf championship. On that memorable afternoon he lost the Amateur title to my old friend, Harrison (Jimmy) Johnson of St. Paul.

A few weeks back, I met Doc in deadly combat on one of the beautiful golf courses in Portland. I had an ace in the hole in Lester Bolstad, noted Minnesota amateur. When the smoke of battle cleared, Bolstad had a par 72, the mighty Doc had a 75, and my son Roger had a 94. My score? Well, nobody but an ill-bred son of a snuse hound would be ignorant enough to inquire about that. –Captain Billy, July 1933

NOT BAD, LESTER BOLSTAD

Local Boy Picks Himself Movie Queen

After turning professional, Lester served as a pro at Westwood Hills, Minneapolis Golf Club, and Golden Valley Country Club before taking over the reins of the University of Minnesota golf team in 1946, a position he would hold for the next 30 years. After a distinguished playing career, Les would spend the second half of his life as a well-respected and innovative teacher. Seventy years before golf teaching looked at the physics of the golf swing, before Trackman and before the Golfing Machine, Les Bolstad was using terms like curvilinear, velocity, sequence, stimulus-response-kinesthesia, leverage, and momentum in his teaching. He based his instruction on Sir Isaac Newton's third law of motion: For every action, there is an equal and opposite reaction.

While basing his teaching on physics, Les would keep his

communication with students simple. A beginning female golfer might be told, "Your swing is still in the backyard. Think about your front yard and your kitchen." World Golf Hall of Fame member Patty Berg remembers her teacher of 45 years giving her the same advice whenever her swing was off. "Tempo, timing, and rhythm, Patricia Jane," Coach Bolstad would always remind her. Throughout her career, the Hall of Fame golfer would use a simple drill Bolstad gave her to help her find her swing. Patty would practice swinging the club with her left hand only, and then, without stopping, put her right hand on the club as she continued to swing over and over—tempo, timing, and rhythm. Make the complex simple.

In a 1976 interview with *Minneapolis Star Tribune* sports columnist Larry Batson, University of Minnesota golfer Dave Haberle gave a wonderful description of coach Bolstad's style of teaching. "Les is a wonderful, loveable old gentleman. He is very kind, generous, and thoughtful. He is kind of spacy at times. He can straighten you out and confuse you at the same time, the way he skips around. But it all means something. If you do not get it all immediately, you get enough to help. Later, when you sort it out, it makes sense. All of his angles have parallels if you follow me."

Dick Williams agrees with Haberle's assessment. Williams played for Les Bolstad in the early 1970s before embarking on a career in golf that included stints as a golf professional and greens superintendent at the Brainerd Country Club and Black Bear Golf Course in Pine River. Dick remembers the detailed precision Bolstad applied to teaching everything from the grip to alignment, and to the swing itself. "I wish I had paid more attention to what he was saying," he recalls. "Most of us would listen to him and then go back to what we were doing before." Dick remembers Bolstad telling him to aim at the Quercus Alba (white oak tree) on a particular hole, and pick out a branch and then a leaf on the branch to focus on. Visualization. As a sniper would say, aim small, miss small.

The mark of a great teacher is someone whose work stands the test of time. For over 50 years, Les Bolstad did not deviate from his teaching principles. In researching his golf instruction, I have found that what Les taught Patty Berg and others in the 1930s was the same thing Dave Haberle and others heard from him in the 1970s.

In 1976, Bolstad said, "Golf is a lifetime learning process. One must have a method and a system that will be effective on days when your 'feel' deserts you. The most common form of instruction is by tips or breaking the swing into parts. We teach a pattern. A golfer should have an order of movement, a definite posture, a definite pattern."

Les retired as a professor and golf coach at the University of Minnesota in 1976. In 1983, the University Golf Course was renamed the Les Bolstad Golf Course. However, Bolstad was not content to ride off into the sunset when he retired. Any Friday morning during the summer, he could be found at his honorary home club, Hazeltine National, helping run the junior golf program. No doubt his students learned more than just how to swing a golf club.

Minnesota businessman and former University of Minnesota golfer Harvey McKay recalls Bolstad teaching him the art of visualization—to see the shot before you hit it—and how he used that principle to become successful in business: "Visualization isn't wishful thinking," McKay said. "It is not daydreaming. It is very serious business. Indispensable to success. I thought Les was teaching me golf lessons. He was teaching me life lessons."

Patricia Jane

The 50th Street Tigers with quarterback Patty Berg (from the collections of the Minnesota Historical Society)

Breezy Point's 1933 tournament also featured the debut performance of Minnesota's most famous female golfer. Patty Berg was born in Minneapolis, Minnesota, on February 13, 1918. Since Patty and I share the same birthday, it is probably not a coincidence that my first golf clubs were a set of Wilson Patty Berg Cup Defenders I borrowed from my mother. Consisting of a brassie (2-wood), spoon (3-wood), 3-, 5-, 7-, and 9-irons, and a putter, the set served me well until I outgrew them and transitioned to a regular men's set.

As a young girl, Patty was a tomboy who enjoyed playing whatever sport was in season, usually with the neighborhood boys. She played quarterback for the 50th Street Tigers, a neighborhood team

68

led by future University of Oklahoma football coach Bud Wilkinson. Berg was the quarterback because she was the only one who could remember the signals. At the age of 13, golf caught her interest. Her father was a member at Interlachen Country Club and signed her up for lessons with golf professional Jim Pringle, who would later serve as golf professional at Breezy Point in the 1940s.

Patty Berg and Les Bolstad sharing a laugh together in 1978.

Patty's first tournament experience in the 1933 Minneapolis City Ladies Championship was painful, as she shot a score of 122 and finished last in the last flight. The next year, all she did was eat, sleep, and play golf. She returned the following year to claim medalist honors and win the ladies' championship. Berg also began taking lessons from four-time Ten Thousand Lakes champion Les Bolstad, who turned pro in 1934. Bolstad gave her an understanding of her golf swing so she could correct herself during a round if necessary. They also spent a lot of time chipping and putting to improve her ability to score on and around the green. Their teacher-student relationship would continue for the next forty years.

Les Bolstad got his first look at Patty at the Ten Thousand Lakes Golf Tournament in Breezy Point. In 1933, the 15-year-old Berg was the sweetheart of the gallery as she defeated six-time defending champion Minnie Little in the semifinals and another young Interlachen golfer, Betty Hays, in the final match to claim the first of her three Ten Thousand Lakes titles. Her match with Dorothy Lanpher in 1934 was one of the best ladies' finals in tournament history. Patty shot an 81 to set a new women's course record at Breezy Point. She needed to play that well, as Ms. Lanpher nearly matched her with an 83. Berg won the match 2 & 1. Patty came back to win three in a row the next year, setting a new course record in qualifying with an 80, even par for ladies at Breezy Point. Clearly superior to the rest of the ladies at the ripe old age of 17, she was never threatened in match play.

Ms. Berg was about to burst out on the national scene. The 1935 U.S. Amateur was played at her home course, Interlachen, and her putter got hot. In the quarterfinals, she made a curving 45-foot putt to advance. In the semifinals, she faced a twisting 25-footer on the 18th green to send the match to extra holes. It was the same putt Bobby Jones made to win the 1930 U.S. Open at Interlachen. Patty holed the putt and went on to win the match on the third extra hole. The 17-year-old would play five-time champion Glenna Collett Vare for the title.

Patty Berg and Stan Larson,
1935 Breezy Point champions

In the 36-hole final, Berg continued to make putts from every-where, thrilling the large and mostly local gallery. At the 32nd hole, Berg was three holes down when she rolled in an 18-footer to take the hole. Patty birdied the next hole as well, but Vare's experience took over as she matched Berg's birdie and birdied the following hole to win the championship 3 & 2. Asked to rank all the fine young golfers at the 1935 amateur, Mrs. Vare said, "By all means Patty Berg first. In fact, quite a distance ahead of the rest, and they were all good."

Patty won her Minnesota Women's Amateur titles in 1935, 1936, and 1938. She would finally go on to win the U.S. Women's Amateur in 1938 along with the Women's Western Amateur and the Trans-Mississippi to become the first golfer to win all three major women's events in the same year. Two years later, after her sophomore year at the University of Minnesota, she made the de-cision to turn pro. There was no professional organization for women golfers at that time, only five women who were well-known pros, and only two tournaments to play in, the Western Open, and the Titleholders. What was available was the chance to represent golf equipment companies and give golf clinics to push their merchandise. That would be Patty's future.

It was also what she excelled at. Representing Wilson Golf, she used a running line of jokes, a collection of wild hats, and the ability to hit any shot on command to bring the game of golf to the American public. Her contract with Wilson was a six-year deal that paid her $7,500 a year. It lasted for 66 years! Like Walter Hagen before her, Patty Berg would put on over 10,000 clinics and exhibitions throughout her career and affiliation with Wilson Golf. Berg would later say, "It was a great, great lesson for me. While promoting the game of golf to men and women, it was the children there who got to see how wonderful golf could be for them." Patty loved to see the smiles she helped put on their faces.

In 1941, Patty teamed up with former Washburn High School classmate and 50th Street neighbor Otis Dypwick to write the book *Golf.* The book was remarkable for its time because of the number of high-quality pictures Otis took of Berg's golf swing. Dypwick co-wrote books with many other professional golfers, including Byron Nelson, Sam Snead, Arnold Palmer, and Gary Player. Otis and Patty teamed up again in 1942 for a follow-up book, *Want to Be a Champion?* They remained lifelong friends.

Along the way, Patty Berg was part of a group of 13 women who gathered in 1949 to start the Ladies Professional Golf Association (LPGA). Berg would serve as the organization's first president from 1950 to 1952. Today, female golfers from around the world compete on the LPGA Tour for over $70 million in prize money. During her professional career, Patty won 60 tournaments and a record 15 major championships, including the first U.S. Women's Open in 1946. She was named the Associated Press Woman Athlete of the Year in three different decades. Patty is a member of the Minnesota Golf Hall of Fame and was also in the original class inducted into the World Golf Hall of Fame in 1974. Not bad for an ex-quarterback!

Although only 5 feet 2 inches tall with red hair and freckles, Patty Berg stood tall in the world of golf for over 60 years. She was all things to women's golf—one of its best players, a tireless promoter, and a timeless teacher with a personality that endeared her to everyone who crossed her path. Part Walter Hagen and part Arnold Palmer, hers was an extraordinary life!

Clint Russell—World Champion Blind Golfer

Clint Russell with caddie Jimmy Koehler

As a youngster, I always remembered what a treat it was to stop at Bridgeman's Ice Cream Shoppe whenever we made a trip to the Twin Cities. After checking the available choices, I would get three scoops of my favorite flavor, Rum Cherry, on a big cone and try to make it last as long as possible. Bridgeman's was an offshoot of the Bridgeman-Russell Dairy Production Company started in Duluth, Minnesota, by Clint Russell's father, Newall Russell, and Henry Bridgeman in 1892. After graduating from college, Clint went to work for the company. An accident in 1924 would change his life forever. On his way home from a hunting trip, his car had a flat tire. While changing the tire, it blew up in Russell's face, leaving him blind.

Several years later, while on vacation in California, his family encouraged him to take a few swings with a golf club. Clint had some success hitting the golf ball and decided to take up the game in earnest when he returned home. Russell developed a system that involved having a caddie tee up his ball, adjust his stance, and line up the club face before each shot. In 1934, he shot an 84 for 18 holes at Duluth's Ridgeview Country Club. Russell was featured in *Ripley's Believe It or Not* along with another blind golfer from England who also had recorded scores of 85 or better. In 1938, Robert Ripley sponsored a match between Clint Russell and W.H.J. Oxenham, the blind English golfer. The match took place on August 24, 1938, at Ridgeview Country Club in Duluth and saw Russell defeat Oxenham 6 & 5 to claim the title as champion blind golfer of the world.

Four days later, Clint and his wife were at Breezy Point for the Upper Midwest Ice Cream Convention. An exhibition match was arranged between Russell and Hollywood actor and resort guest Wayne Morris. Morris was at Breezy Point as a guest of owner Billy Fawcett. It was the first time Clint had played the golf course, and the absence of his regular caddie—who supervised his stance, angled his club, and in other ways acted as his eyes—caused him trouble on a few holes. Russell piled up an early lead until Morris reined in his wild slice to pull out a 1-up victory over the blind golfer in their nine-hole match. Clint recorded a score of 58 to the actor's 54. A large gallery from the ice cream convention at Breezy Point was on hand following the golfers.

Scorecard from the Russell-Morris exhibition

Les Bolstad, Wayne Morris, and Captain Billy Fawcett

Clint Russell went on to win the National Blind Golfer Championship in 1946 and the International Invitational Blind Golfer Tournament in 1947 and 1948. He inspired many blind people to give golf a try and helped form the United States Blind Golf Association in 1953. Russell received the 1956 Ben Hogan Award, presented annually to the golfer who has made the greatest comeback from illness or injury. In 1975, he was enshrined in the Duluth Arena Sports Hall of Fame.

John Montague: Man of Mystery— Walter Hagen returns to Breezy Point

Most people went to Hollywood in the 1930s hoping to find their way into the limelight. One man went there in hopes of avoiding it. In August of 1930, LaVerne Moore was part of a robbery gone bad in upstate New York. During a high-speed chase with the police, one of the robbers died, two of them were captured, and a fourth vanished into thin air, leaving behind a set of golf clubs and papers that identified him as LaVerne Moore. Five foot ten inches tall and weighing 220 pounds, the man from Syracuse, New York, was a natural athlete who had almost superhuman strength. It was a perfect combination for golf: strong enough to hit a golf ball prodigious distances with the athletic finesse to score on and around the green. Now he was gone, and no one seemed to know where he was.

John Montague showed up in Hollywood in the early 1930s. Nobody knew where he came from, where he lived, or how he made his money. He played golf at Lakeside Golf Club along with many of the stars of Hollywood; Johnny Weissmuller of Tarzan fame, Babe Hardy of the Laurel and Hardy team (Montague's roommate for a time), Dick Arlen, Guy Kibbe, and billionaire Howard Hughes were all members at Lakeside. Bing Crosby was a four-time club champion there. It was a crowd Breezy Point's Billy Fawcett would have been comfortable hanging around with. He knew most of them personally, and probably either knew or had heard of this Montague character as well.

Monty won the club championship at Lakeside in 1933 and 1934. He and Crosby would frequently play matches against each other. One such match had a rather interesting twist. *Desert Sun* sports columnist Braven Dyer gave Bing's account of what happened in an article he wrote for the October 1971 *Professional Golfer Magazine*:

> "After we had finished playing one afternoon," recalls Der Bingle, "we were at the bar, arguing, as golfers will, about proper handicaps. Monty said he could beat me, using a bat, a shovel, and a rake. This appealed to me, if for no other reason than it was an outlandish proposal, and I offered to take him up on it at five dollars a hole." (Several Lakeside members claimed it was for $1,000 a hole, but Montague refused to reveal what they played for, and Crosby insisted it was only $5).

> Crosby grinned as he went on with his story. "We went to the tenth tee at Lakeside, and he produced a fungo bat, threw the ball up in the air, and hit it a prodigious wallop. It rolled into the bunker, directly in front of the green, a distance of about 350 yards from the tee."

> "I bumped a girlish effort down the fairway about 210 yards and then threw it up on the green about fifteen feet away

from the hole with a 7-iron. Montague then produced a shovel, strode into the bunker, and shoveled the ball up onto the green about six feet from the hole."

"I putted first and missed. He then took a rake, turned it upside down and, with the back of the rake, pushed it in for birdie three. I had seen enough, and we went back to the bar for a little more conviviality."

As a young golfer, I remember trying all kinds of trick shots with my friends. How many times could I bounce a golf ball on the face of my clubhead? Could I hook a ball around a tree, or slice it in the opposite direction? One of my friends found his ball up against a tree with no chance to swing at it from the right side. When he asked me how I would play that shot, I dropped a ball next to the tree, turned my 8-iron upside down, and hit the ball left-handed onto the green 100 yards away!

Our favorite contest involved playing a hole with only one club, which forced us to be highly creative. I usually chose a 6-iron to play all my shots, but my teammate Greg Peterson would use his mallet head putter to drive the ball 180-plus yards, bump the next shot up by the green, and usually get up and down for his four. All these trick shots helped us to develop the eye-hand coordination every good golfer needs. Trick shots were fun to try; they stretched our imagination and helped us to think "outside the box."

Montague was not just a trick-shot artist. He could really play and set several course records at different California courses. One week in Palm Springs, he shot consecutive rounds of 61, 61, 61, and 58 while playing with actor Dick Arlen. The great American sportswriter Grantland Rice spent the winter months in Southern California and played quite often at Lakeside. After watching

Monty play a few times, he wrote an article claiming he had found the next great American golfer. *TIME* magazine followed up on that and had some pictures taken without Montague's knowledge. When the article and pictures were published in January of 1937, police officers in New York spotted the similarity between the mysterious Montague and their robbery suspect, LaVerne Moore. Admitting that he was the long-lost Moore, Montague was arrested and transported back to New York to stand trial. He was eventually found innocent of the charges after a long, controversial trial featuring several of Monty's Hollywood friends as character witnesses.

No longer having to hide, Montague decided to try and cash in on his newfound fame. He tried playing the PGA Tour but could no longer shoot the scores he was famous for. Monty had lost almost 50 yards in distance and no longer had that safecracker's touch around the greens. The trial had taken a toll on him physically and mentally, and he no longer had the desire or drive to improve that successful PGA players had. Eventually, he was left playing a series of meaningless exhibition matches as he and Walter Hagen barnstormed across the country.

The last week of July 1939 brought the two golfers to Minnesota for the St. Paul Open at Keller Golf Course. Hagen and Montague, two of the gallery favorites, were paired together during the first two rounds of the tournament. The Haig drew a laugh from the crowd on the fifth hole Saturday. Monty had just driven his ball when—*whiz!*—another ball took off within yards of his and followed it right down the fairway. It was a prank by Hagen, who took his windup while Montague wasn't looking and swung a second after the burly Californian. Dick Metz won $1,600 with his first-place score of 270. Four-time Ten Thousand Lakes champion Les Bolstad finished in the money with a 291. Hagen, with a score of

293, and Montague, with 299, finished out of the money.

Following the St. Paul tournament, the two golfers traveled north for an exhibition match at Breezy Point GC on Thursday afternoon. Hagen would use regulation golf clubs, while Montague would strut his stuff with a bat, a shovel, and a rake. The match would settle once and for all the superiority of either the orthodox or the bizarre in golf implements. It was a production made-to-order for Breezy Point's Billy Fawcett. The match caused quite a controversy, as the UP wire report from August 4 recounted:

Breezy Point, MN, Aug. 4 (United Press)
Groundskeepers at the Breezy Point golf course roamed the greens and fairways today, replacing divots dug yesterday when 'Mysterious' John Montague, armed with shovel, rake, and baseball bat, matched strokes for nine holes with veteran Walter Hagen. Hagen, using his regulation clubs, could do no better than tie the unorthodox Montague, both golfers carding 33's.

The actual match, however, was an anti-climax compared to the labor trouble which preceded it. When it was learned that Montague was to use the rake and shovel, Groundskeeper Elmer Erickson of the Breezy Point course threatened to re-sign, claiming that his beautifully kept fairways and greens would be spoiled. Then, accompanying Erickson's mutiny by presenting a united front, the entire caddy force at the course refused to work, foreseeing there would be too much labor in replacing the divots dug by Montague's garden tools.

Manager Allen Adams, however, shoved two husky University of Minnesota football players, John Mariucci and Chuck

Myre, into the carrying breech. The muscular 'scabs' toted the equipment for the two golfers but were jeered and hooted by the regular caddies. Incidentally, the score, 33, set a new course record- for shovel and rake golfers!

According to Capt. Billy Fawcett, the two will remain at Breezy Point over the weekend for a fishing trip. They also will make suggestions on improving the golf course, in keeping with the general rebuilding program going on at the resort.

Billy Fawcett had a tradition of offering summer employment to select University of Minnesota athletes. A hundred dollars a month plus room and board was the standard rate. Mariucci and Myre were no doubt part of that crew. It should be noted that "caddie" John Mariucci went on to play professional hockey with the Chicago Blackhawks from 1940 to 1952 and later coached the U of M hockey team from 1952 to 1966. He is known as the "Godfather of Minnesota Hockey" and was inducted into the United States Hockey Hall of Fame with the 1973 inaugural class. In the 1970s, he came back to the Brainerd area as part of the Camp Confidence Celebrity Golf Tournament. "Maroosh" put on the Mariucci Fiesta Italian Dinner Saturday nights for all the participants and contributors. The dinner and silent auction raised thousands of dollars each year for the Camp Confidence Learning Center.

As for the mysterious Montague, there was no more mystery. Too much food and a dependence on alcohol took a toll on his body as he once again faded from the limelight, this time not by choice. His life slowly came to an end until he passed away in May of 1972. As the poet T. S. Eliot would have said, "Not with a bang, but a whimper." RIP, Monty!

Hagen, Montague at Breezy

Walter Hagen and John Montague, two of the outstanding professional golfers in the nation, exhibited their wares before over 300 spectators at Breezy Point's sporty nine-hole course yesterday afternoon. Posing for the picture above are, left to right: Walter Hagen, Minnesota football players John Mariucci and Chuck Myre, and John Montague. Included in the afternoon's program were various trick shots by Montague, who used a baseball bat and shovel as part of his golfing equipment. August 4, 1939.

Picture from the 1939 exhibition signed by Walter Hagen and John Montague

Chapter 4: The War to End All Wars

In January of 1940, Captain Billy came down with a cold while on his way to Hollywood from New York. He was hospitalized in Hollywood with pneumonia but died three weeks later on February 7, 1940, of heart disease. Funeral services were held in Minneapolis, and he was buried at Lakewood Cemetery next to his brother, Captain Roscoe Fawcett, who had died two years earlier.

Billy Fawcett's boys took over the management of Breezy Point. It was business as usual for a couple of years until America found itself pulled into another war. The resort was closed in 1942, with only a maintenance crew working for the next few years. The Breezy Point Golf Course got a rest as most golfers were either in the service or helping out with the war effort at home. The resort was offered to both the Army and Navy for use as a military base with no strings attached, but no one took them up on the offer.

Before long, America was fighting a war on two fronts in both the Atlantic and Pacific. In the 1930s, Harry Truman was a colonel in the Army Reserves who regularly trained at Fort Ripley, just south of Brainerd. This put him near one of his favorite spots, Breezy Point. Harry liked to play the slots and was known to hit the jackpot a time or two while visiting Breezy. Truman became president of the United States after Franklin Roosevelt's death in

1945. No longer dropping coins in the slots, Truman instead dropped the atomic bomb on Japan in 1946. Jackpot! The war was over.

As the war was winding down, the Fawcett boys were busy with their publishing empire, creating a new hero—Captain Marvel—who is still doing quite well today. Not as emotionally tied to the resort as their father was, they decided the time had come to sell. On Monday, September 11, 1944, while Allied forces were driving the German troops back in an all-out retreat and President Roosevelt and England's Prime Minister Winston Churchill were meeting in Quebec, Canada, to plan the ultimate defeat of the Axis forces, a pending sale of Breezy Point to hotel owners Fred and Rush McAllister was being announced. The sale did not go through. It was not until August of 1945 that Breezy Point was finally sold to Theron "Tiny" Holmes, a Coca-Cola distributor from Brainerd. The resort opened again in the summer of 1946, featuring music by big-name bands each weekend. Clark Gable and Gene Autry were both seen vacationing at the resort.

Jim Pringle, former assistant at Interlachen, was hired as head golf professional and put in charge of getting the golf course back in playing shape. The Ten Thousand Lakes Tournament returned in 1946 after a four-year absence. Gene Wright, home on leave from the Coast Guard, shot 76 to lead the qualifiers in the 1946 tournament. Along with his brother Frank, Gene made up the famous golfing "Wright Brothers" from Brainerd. Wright had little trouble winning his first three matches and faced F. S. Brinkman of Tulsa, Oklahoma, in the finals. Gene shot a 36 on the first nine holes to take a 1-up lead on Brinkman, who went out in 38. Wright was two up going into the 17th when Brinkman's tee shot found water on the left, allowing Wright to close out their match 3 & 1. It would be eight years before the tournament was played again.

85

Holmes ran the resort for two years before selling it to Jack Salenger of Chicago and his silent partner, Brownie Cote, owner of nearby Grand View Lodge.

Horter McVeigh

Horter McVeigh, age 19, took over the reins at Breezy Point as their golf professional in 1940. From Hollywood, California, he started playing golf when he was 13, turned pro at the age of 16, and worked at Sunset Fields CC in Los Angeles before coming to Breezy Point in 1940.

He was a promising young player and a protégé of the great MacDonald Smith. PGA champion Paul Runyan thought that McVeigh, among all the young golfers being developed in the 1930s, had the best chance to equal the deeds of Bobby Jones. Horter played on the winter PGA Tour in 1939, '40, and '41, competing alongside the likes of Sam Snead, Byron Nelson, and Ben Hogan.

"That's an experience which makes one realize that golf is a tough game," he related to the *LA Times'* Charles Curtis in 1940. "I realize that I'm biting off a big chew in trying to compete against America's greatest playing pros," he said, "but at the same time, if I can win, this achievement will be worth plenty to me." At the 1940 St. Paul Open won by Ed "Porky" Oliver, McVeigh finished in the money (top 20) with a score of 290. Snead shot 280, and Hogan a 281.

The Fourth of July was always a special time at Breezy Point and usually involved some kind of golf competition that was a little out of the ordinary. On July 4, 1940, Breezy Point offered a nine-hole golf jamboree under the direction of new golf professional

Horter McVeigh. On July 3, 1940, the *Sioux City Journal* carried this news release from Breezy Point:

The time has come when even the worst dub can take up clubs against the finest pro. And all because of the jamboree of goofy golf to be held at Breezy Point on the Fourth of July. Teeing off from wavy, rubber hoses, shooting through barrels, plopping balls into buckets of water- these are but a few of the fun hazards that will line Breezy's nine-hole course. Not only these, but free beer at every tee will add to the merriment. The best possible description, however, would be a brief recital of the jamboree program.

Hole 1- **Surprise Hole**- Play as instructed

Hole 2- **The Dizzy Dean**- Throw ball from tee and play the balance of the hole with PUTTER.

Hole 3- **The Ku Klux Klan**- Tee up ball, take stance, then place hood overhead and do the best you can. GREEN- cushion billiards. Putt for holes in front of board; if a player puts ball through holes with even number, he adds this number to his score. If odd number, he deducts from score.

Hole 4- **The Zebra Zone**- If drive stops between 135 and 150 markers, ADD one stroke; between 165 and 180, no penalty; between 180 and 200, ADD one stroke; between 200 and 215, no penalty; between 215 and green, ADD two strokes. GREEN- chip ball into tub. If you fail after 3 tries pick up and ADD two strokes.

Hole 5- **The Can-Can**- Place both feet in cans and tee ball up on rubber hose. Use wood club to green. GREEN- Putt to nearest hole.

Hole 6- **The Corrigan**- Drive with No. 8 iron. Second with No. seven iron. Third with No. 6 iron. Fourth with No. 5 iron. Then use a wood club to the green. GREEN- use a billiard cue.

Breezy's professional Horter McVeigh competes in the Golf Jamboree

Hole 7- **Snake Eyes**- Roll dice furnished. You lie from the tee what you roll.

Hole 8- **The Babe Ruth**- Use baseball bat from the tee. Free cigars will be given for all home runs- beyond 300 yards. Play the rest of the hole crosshanded.

Hole 9- **The Tippler**- Place ball in paper cup furnished. Drive with regular club. All who hit the target may deduct 10 strokes. GREEN- use marbles furnished, knuckle into the cup

After another winter on the PGA Tour, Horter took an assistant pro position at Red Run GC in Detroit in 1941. On July 23, 1941, returning from a party in honor of his twenty-first birthday, Horter McVeigh drove his car into a streetlamp post. He was pronounced dead at the scene of the accident. Sadly, we will never know how good he might have been.

Ladies' Golf at Breezy Point

The anacronym G.O.L.F. (Gentlemen Only, Ladies Forbidden) has never been in vogue at Breezy Point. From the first Ten Thousand Lakes Tournament in 1924, owner Billy Fawcett and director of all things golf, Roscoe Fawcett, always included a women's division as part of the tournament. Fawcett family friend Minerva "Minnie" Little won the ladies' title six times in the first nine years the tournament was held. The most notable winner in the tournament's history was a woman, World Golf Hall of Fame member Patty Berg. Patty won at Breezy Point three times between 1933 and 1935. Her 1933 victory at the age of 15 was the first time she ever won a golf tournament. Berg would go on to win over 90 times, including 15 women's major championships.

Patty Berg at Breezy Point in 1933

Mrs. Owen Safford won the ladies' division of the Ten Thousand Lakes Golf Tournament in 1927 and 1928, interrupting a seven-year run where Mrs. Ralph Little claimed the championship five times. During her career, Mrs. Safford was the editor and publisher of a sports magazine, author of a cookbook (*Food of My Friends*), and a member of the Shubert Stock Company acting troupe in Minneapolis. Virginia began writing for the *Minneapolis Star* in 1939 and wrote a regular travel, society, and food column for the paper until retiring in 1953.

Mrs. Safford was active in sports and won city golf and swimming championships. Her brother, Jake Weatherby, was an accomplished golfer who finished runner-up to Les Bolstad in the Ten Thousand Lakes Tournament in 1930. Playing out of Minneapolis Golf Club, brother Jake finished runner-up to Minnesota's champion golfer, Jimmy Johnson, in the State Amateur in 1922 and 1926 as well. Weatherby went by the nickname "Mountain Jake," and not because of his size. Before the advent of the wooden tee, golfers would pinch a clump of sand together to form a tee for driving their golf ball. Jake made his mound of sand so big it looked like his ball was sitting on top of a small mountain, hence the nickname.

Golfer and Sportsman magazine was a monthly periodical published and edited by Virginia Safford in Minneapolis, primarily covering the social scene in the western suburbs of Minneapolis but including St. Paul and other parts of the state. The subscription rate was $1 per year, or 15 cents an issue. In 1927, Billy Fawcett introduced a new magazine based on *Golfer and Sportsman* with Mrs. Safford's help and expertise. The *Brainerd Dispatch* reported on May 13, 1927: "We have on our desk today the first issue of Captain William H. Fawcett's new golf magazine, *The 10,000 Lakes Golfer and Outdoor Magazine*. It covers the field in a comprehensive manner, and we are especially pleased to see the prominence accorded golf news from Brainerd." The new golf magazine was put together with Mrs. Safford in charge as general manager, Hubert Dustin as editor, and Leon Pilon Jr. as business manager. Beautiful artwork by Frances Buholz graced the magazine's cover each month.

The 10,000 Lakes Golfer, a Billy Fawcett/
Virginia Safford collaboration.

Mrs. Safford provided coverage of the Ten Thousand Lakes Tournament each year along with pictures of golfers competing and people out watching the golfers.

Mrs. Ralph Little, six-time Ten Thousand Lakes ladies champion.

Delores Del Rio, Clair Winsor, and Antoinette Fawcett
in the gallery at Breezy in 1931

Edith Kierland of Alexandria won the ladies' title at Breezy in 1936. Edith was also an eight-time Resorters champion. She won the Alexandria Resorters title five times in a row from 1931 to 1935 and claimed her last Resorters title in 1949. Kierland was hard to beat on her home course. Edith won the last two holes in her match against Gertrude Andressen to capture the Ten Thousand Lakes title in 1936.

Edith Kierland shows her form off the tee.

Ann Haroldson of Duluth was the ladies' champion at Breezy Point in 1937, one year after losing out to Patty Berg in the Minnesota Women's State Amateur. Haroldson was a professional skater who was a star for the Ice Follies in the 1930s. Ann checked with golf officials before becoming a professional skater to make sure she could still compete as an amateur in golf. She played in several state events in the '30s and '40s but only played one time at Breezy Point.

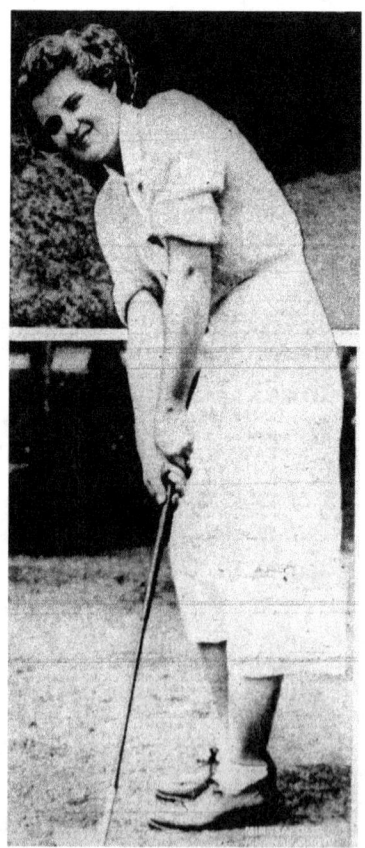

1937 ladies champion Ann Haroldson

College Golfers Compete
at Breezy Point

1937 champion Maurice Cain and runner-up Neil Croonquist

Beginning in 1937, college golfers began to dominate the Ten Thousand Lakes Tournament. In 1937, it was an all-North Dakota final after Neil Croonquist of Bismark defeated Bob Shay one up, and Maurice Cain of Wahpeton held off John Buck 2 & 1 in their semifinal matches. The final match featured two big-time college players, with Cain a member of the University of Southern California golf team and Croonquist the number-one player for the University of Minnesota's Big Ten championship team. Maurice Cain prevailed in the final match by a score of 4 & 2. Maurice also won the Resorters in 1936 and the Birchmont and Pine to Palm in 1938 to become the first golfer to complete the resort tournament "Grand Slam": the Birchmont, Ten Thousand Lakes, Resorters, and Pine to Palm tournaments. Cain defeated Croonquist 2 & 1 in the finals of his Pine to Palm victory as well. Don't feel too bad for Neil Croonquist, though. Neil won his first Minnesota State Amateur in 1941 and repeated nineteen years later, the longest lapse between titles in MGA Amateur history. A year after losing to Cain at Detroit Lakes, he came back to win the Pine to Palm in 1939. He was a four-time winner at the Resorters, claiming the title in 1953, 1957, 1964, and 1975. That means Croonquist won a major state golf championship in five different decades. We may never see that happen again.

In 1938, the first-round match everyone wanted to see matched Babe LeVoir against Bud Wilkinson in a battle of former Minnesota Gophers football teammates. LeVoir prevailed and went on to face medalist John Buck in the semifinals, where Babe won again in a match of long-ball hitters 4 & 3. Rivals Bobby Campbell and Harry Robinson met in the other semifinal contest, where Campbell emerged with a 1-up victory. The *Minneapolis Star*'s golf correspondent, Bernard Swanson, was on hand to describe the final match:

> "Babe LeVoir has played golf seriously for only the last two years and this week was his first venture into tournament play. He all but caught Bobby Campbell, certainly the best

shot-maker around here. It took consecutive birdies on the tenth and eleventh holes and a three-under-par salvo the whole route to slap down Babe's ears, and when anyone is playing wee Bobby that close, he's playing lots of golf. It's a sight to see the Babe hit them. His drive off the tee is a low, whistling ball that barely clears the grass when it takes off. The popular expression at Breezy Point was 'Have you seen that Babe LeVoir hit em?' His play to the green isn't too good yet, but that's the result of inexperience and resulted in a 3 & 2 decision for Campbell."

Babe LeVoir and Bobby Campbell

In 1939, Kansas University's Dean Ritchie and state junior champion Wally Ulrich of Austin tied for medalist honors with scores of 75. While his sister Patty recovered from appendectomy surgery, younger brother Herman Berg shot a back-nine 34 to defeat Ritchie 1-up in their first-round match.

1939 champion Herman Berg

In the semifinals, Herman defeated Ernotte Hiller of Crookston 1-up while Emil Sorenson of Topeka, Kansas, defeated 1937 champion Maurice Cain of Wahpeton, North Dakota, by the same margin. Sorenson was no match for Berg in the finals. Herman crashed out three birdies in the last six holes to end the match on 15 when he drained a 20-footer from the edge of the green for a birdie on the 547-yard hole. He consistently outdrove his opponents with a smooth compact swing. The husky, freckle-faced redhead's approaches and putts matched his devastating drives that week. Not yet a college golfer, Berg was the current Minnesota High School champion.

The best of the college players at Breezy Point during this time was Dean Ritchie. The Kansas state amateur champion repeated as medalist in 1940 with a superb round of three-under-par 69. Ritchie defeated Herman Ridder in the semifinals while Ernotte Hiller of Crookston outlasted that year's giant slayer, Walt Hargesheimer, in the other semifinal. Hargesheimer took out two of the tournament favorites, public links finalist Sumner Lind and college champion Gene Christenson, in the first two rounds. Ritchie defeated Hiller 1-up in a closely played final match to capture the Ten Thousand Lakes title. Kansas was but one state represented among the Ten Thousand Lakes competitors. Texas, Oklahoma, California, New York, Missouri, and North and South Dakota also had golfers competing in the tournament, as Northern Minnesota offered a cool respite from the summer heat enveloping the country. Dean Ritchie won medalist honors for the third year in a row in 1941, shooting a 1-under-par 71. The semifinal matches on Sunday featured Ritchie against Chet Nelson and Yale University's number-one player Jim Harris versus Ted McFarland. McFarland defeated one of the favorites, Wally Ulrich of Carleton College, in 21 holes in their quarterfinal match. Ulrich would go on to win the

National Collegiate golf championship in 1943 and four Minnesota Opens as a pro in 1946, 1947, 1951, and 1955. Wally played on the PGA Tour in the 1950s and was among the top 30 money winners in 1953. Ritchie beat Nelson 2 & 1 in the morning, while Harris defeated McFarland 3 & 1. The Kansas ace was 1-under-par going out against Harris in the finals to grab a 3-up lead. He then played even par for the next six holes to win on the 15th green, 4 & 3, and claim his second Ten Thousand Lakes championship.

Ten Thousand Lakes champion Dean Ritchie, on the right,
with two-time Pine Beach champion Joe Ryan

Chapter 5: The Post-War Boom

The 1950s produced the generation known as the Baby Boomers. There were about four million babies born every year in the '50s. The American economy was booming as well. Rates of unemployment and inflation were low, and wages were high. The middle class had more money to spend. Families began moving out of the city to what would be called the suburbs, where modest inexpensive housing was being mass-produced. Pastel colors like pink, mint green, turquoise, and pale yellow were now the choices offered by interior designers. The G.I. Bill subsidized low-cost mortgages for returning soldiers. These suburban homes were perfect for young families looking for room to grow. Many were even able to find some extra money to purchase land and build a small cabin on a Northern Minnesota lake for a weekend getaway.

Life was good in the 1950s, as long as you weren't a Communist. An anti-Communist "Red Scare" was used to chase so-called Communist sympathizers out of government, schools, and even Hollywood. Communism needed to be contained, which drew America into what President Truman called a "police action" in Korea and became the Korean War. The '50s also saw the birth of rock and roll, as well as the civil rights and women's rights movements, which reached their peak in the next decade.

Breezy Point went through several owners in the 1950s, none with pockets as deep as Captain Billy Fawcett. In 1955, Jack Salenger, who had purchased Breezy Point in 1948, sold a substantial interest in the resort to his silent partner, R.F. "Brownie" Cote of Grand View Lodge, and general manager Ken Kellar. Cote and Kellar announced plans for a $100,000 expansion program which would include improvements to the golf course. The green on hole six was moved back to the top of the hill by the clubhouse, changing it from a par-5 to a 375-yard par-4. The nine-hole course would now play to a par of 35. In addition, they would be bringing back the Ten Thousand Lakes Golf Tournament after a 10-year lapse. On August 19, many of the state's top players returned to Breezy Point for the 16th playing of the match-play tournament.

Roy Widstrom of Los Angeles, California, was medalist with a three-under-par 67. In an exciting final match, Widstrom defeated Kenny Young of Interlachen 1-up in 19 holes. Roy held a 2-up advantage through 16, but Young rallied to win 17 and 18 with a birdie and a par. Widstrom then fired a birdie on the first extra hole to take the title.

1955 Ten Thousand Lakes medalist and champion, Roy Widstrom, was an offbeat, multifaceted individual. A World War II bomber pilot credited with flying 38 missions, Widstrom was a master bridge player who played semi-pro football in his younger days and drove a cab later in life. He was an Arthur Murray dance instructor for several years and won a national teaching award for dance in 1954. While living in California in the 1950s, Roy played number-one man for the University of San Francisco golf team and competed against the likes of Ken Venturi and Harvie Ward in the prestigious San Francisco City Championship. Widstrom played some of his best golf later in life. He won the Brainerd Shortstop tournament in 1970 with a five-under-par score of 102

for 27 holes. Roy won three consecutive Minnesota Senior Amateur titles between 1973 and 1975. His two Chippewa Valley Senior
titles included a 66 in 1981 and a 67 in 1985, which allowed him to
shoot his age for the first time.

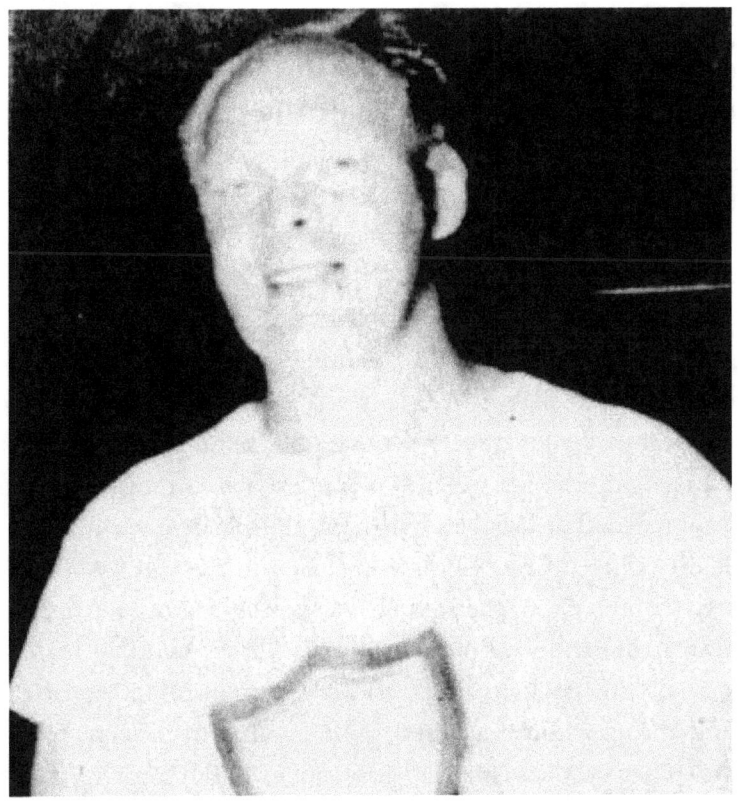

A powerful hitter with an awkward style, Widstrom said dancing was the key to his golf swing. He claimed that the hip motion
of the rumba did more for his golf swing than 100 hours of hitting
practice balls. An integral part of the rumba is the rolling of the
hips, known as the "Cuban Motion." The steps for the dance
mimic the weight shift in a golf swing.

For the rest of the 1950s, Breezy Point's ownership resembled football's triple-reverse, double-handoff option play. Brownie Cote sold his interest to Ken Kellar in 1956 under a contract for deed. Ken assigned the contract back to Jack Salenger in 1957 when Keller became the owner/operator of Izaty's Lodge on Mille Lacs Lake. Salenger then leased the resort to two of his friends from Illinois, Larry Boyle and Richard Wright, in 1958.

With the many changes in ownership, the one constant at Breezy Point in the 1950s was golf professional Ralph "Red" Ledding. Red started his golf career as a 10-year-old caddie at University Golf Course in 1927, became the caddie master at Minneapolis GC under Gunner Johnson in 1946, and was an assistant pro at Westwood Hills from 1947 to 1948. Ledding then sold golf equipment on the road for various manufacturers from 1950 to 1951 before coming to Breezy as a Class-A PGA professional in 1952. He did not play a lot of competitive golf, as he found himself too busy managing the course and giving lessons to find time to play. Red got married in 1956, and his wife, Earnie, helped run the shop while they were at Breezy Point. An article in the *Minneapolis Tribune* society column that year said she was proving to be a delightful hostess at the Breezy Point clubhouse: "Mrs. Ledding managed, with a soft Mississippi drawl, to keep some semblance of order around the clubhouse as tired golfers came in looking for cool drinks. They've been married just since March and haven't had time for a honeymoon yet—too busy getting the golf club ship-shape for the season." When he was not active at the golf course, Ledding played the drum set in various bands throughout the United States. During the winter of 1949, he formed his own trio for a tour of the West Coast.

In 1961, the Breezy Point golf course was closed for part of the season. Ledding took over a golf course in Menominee, Wisconsin, on a lease agreement. Red brought greenskeeper John Fouth and golf shop assistant Eddie Nickel with him from Breezy to get the golf course in top playing condition. He was hired as the head pro at Birch Bay GC near Gull Lake in 1963, worked at Sundance GC in 1965, and was an assistant pro at Oak Ridge CC in 1966.

Red Ledding, Breezy Point professional from 1952 to 1962

With the help of Billy Fawcett's old friend Otis Dypwick, former manager of the Breezy Point golf course, the Ten Thousand Lakes Tournament continued to attract a strong field throughout the 1950s and '60s. In addition, Art Hays, a Gull Lake summer resident, encouraged a good many of his Interlachen clubmates and other fine golfers from the cities to come up and participate in the Ten Thousand Lakes Tournament during this time. The picture on the next page shows 1956 champion Kenny Young, 1963 and 1967 champion Art Hays, and three-time champion Len Bjorklund. Bjorklund won in 1959, 1960, and 1962. It looks like a friendly bunch, but I wouldn't bet on it!

Interlachen Country Club members competing in the 1956 tournament.

Kenny Young had a distinguished career in Minnesota golf, winning the State Amateur in 1938 along with runner-up finishes in 1948 and 1951. Kenny was also runner-up in the State Open in 1947 and had four other top-five finishes between 1948 and 1961. After losing the championship match in extra holes in 1955, he returned to capture the 1956 trophy with a 3 & 2 victory over Minnesota Public Links champion John Biernat.

The following year featured maybe the best match ever played at Breezy Point. It was a quarterfinal match between medalist Rolf

Deming and John Biernat. Both players shot four-under-par 66s, playing two rounds on the par-35 layout. In 1957, Breezy Point golf consisted of just nine holes, all east of County Highway #4, with some going down below the clubhouse where the channel from Moose-O-Bay would later be dredged. Present Hole Number 8 was Number 8 then as well, but it was a short par-5. A good drive took a player across the clubhouse road and just beyond the present tee.

The match was tight all the way. It seesawed back and forth, with birdies being traded and bogeys few and far between. Deming did win number 18 with a par to draw even and set the stage for the extra-hole finish. Biernat lost no time in hitting up his approach for a "gimme" three on the short par-4 starting hole. Wedge shots and a hot putter carried the day for him. Deming had won the State High School Championship in 1956 and 1957, and the State Junior crown in 1957 as well. Rolf was 5-under-par after qualifying and playing his first-round match, and he found himself in the consolation bracket. Biernat made it to the finals for the second year in a row before running into a buzz saw known as Tom Hadley. Hadley was 6-under-par in their final match, easily winning the title.

Ten Thousand Lakes Tournament director, Otis Dypwick, helped Breezy Point recruit a stellar field for the 1957 tournament. Along with Hadley, Biernat, Deming, and defending champion Kenny Young, veteran resort competitors Bud Chapman, Len Bjorklund, Jim Deeble, Don Peddie, Jack Adams, Art Hays, Paul Stoner, and Stan Olson all competed in the tournament.

The following year was a case of "will they, or won't they?" Sid Hartman reported that Breezy Point Lodge had been sold again in April of 1958. On April 22, golf columnist Jack Goodwin reported there was some doubt if the Ten Thousand Lakes Tournament would be held that year. On June 29, Goodwin reported the tournament had been canceled. Finally, on July 18, Goodwin reported the good news that the tournament was back on.

Kenny Young continued his fine play at Breezy Point, shooting a 2-under-par 68 to claim medalist honors. Quarterfinal matches saw Young defeat Al Lerum 3 & 2, Bill Waryan over Art Hays 3 & 2, Ted Listug of Roseau 2 & 1 over Ole Williamson, and young Jim Pfleider of Anoka outlasting Don Peddie in a match that went 20 holes. In the semifinals, Young defeated Pfleider after 23 holes, and Waryan beat Listug to set up a finals match between the two state champions. Playing over a rain-drenched golf course, Bill Waryan defeated Kenny Young 4 & 3 to claim the 1958 title. Waryan was the 1956 State Amateur champion and the Minnesota Open champion in 1950 and 1959. He is a member of the Minnesota Golf Hall of Fame.

Don Peddie, Al Lerum, and Jim Pfleider watch Kenny Young putt during the 1958 quarterfinal matches.

1958 champion Bill Waryan and runner-up Kenny Young "Swinging in the Rain" during Sunday's final round

A fire on June 20, 1959, destroyed the 37-year-old main lodge that Captain Billy had built at Breezy Point. Two people died and at least 22 were injured while trying to escape the burning building.

Three stories high, the lodge was built of western cedar logs held together with wooden drift pins, a type of construction known only to a few wood craftsmen. The Edgewood Annex located south of the lodge was also destroyed in the blaze. Damage from the fire was estimated at $1.75 million.

Breezy Point's main lodge burns down in 1959.

The resort operators continued to keep Breezy Point open, with 60 cabins remaining that had not been affected by the fire. However, the resort would lose a lot of its convention business without a main lodge available to handle the larger groups. Three weeks after the fire, golfers were teeing off at Breezy Point in the 25th playing of the Ten Thousand Lakes Golf Tournament. Ole Williamson was the medalist of the 1959 tournament with a score of 73 but was defeated by Kenny Young in the first round of match play. Young met fellow Interlachen golfer Art Hays in one semifinal match while another Interlachen member, Len Bjorklund, took on Al Lerum of Minnetonka in the other semifinal. Bjorklund defeated Lerum 5 & 4 while Hays took the measure of former champ Young 3 & 2. In an all-Interlachen final, Bjorklund outlasted Hays 3 & 1 to win the first of his three Ten Thousand Lakes championships.

Len Bjorklund, left, receives congratulations from Art Hays Jr., whom he defeated in the finals of the 1959 Ten Thousand Lakes Golf Tournament.

Paul Bunyan Sports Club at Breezy Point

The Paul Bunyan Sports Club's annual summer party began at Breezy Point in 1952. University of Minnesota coaches, Twin Cities press, and prominent business and professional people from around the state would attend this event to promote the university's sports programs. Some came for the golf.

Athletic Director Ike Armstrong, football coach Wes Fesler, basketball coach Ozzie Cowles, and hockey's John Mariucci did an excellent job selling their department to the Northern Minnesota contingent. Fesler dominated on the golf course, where he was a frequent competitor in the Ten Thousand Lakes Tournament, winning low gross, low net, and low team many times. Like Breezy Point's founder, Captain Billy Fawcett, some came for the trap shooting by the lake.

In 1954, organizers planned to make this a statewide organization that would bring the north and south closer together while promoting sports in Minnesota. The annual event was moved from Breezy Point after the lodge burned down in 1959 but would return for one final soiree in 1962. Finally, some came just for the party.

Caddies at Breezy Point

The word "caddie" had its beginning in the 16th century, when Mary Queen of Scots began playing the game in the company of French page boys who were called "cadets." It was a new word for the Scots, and they mispronounced it as "caddies," giving birth to a new word.

Caddies first appeared in the Brainerd Lakes area with the opening of the Chippewa Links Golf Course at Breezy Point in 1924. In November of 1925, newspapers across the country carried this report:

Big Indian Caddies' "Fore" Easily Heard on Minnesota Links- Pequot Lakes, Minn.

"Yi-yip! Fore!" This resounding cry sometimes echoes across the Breezy Point lodge golf course as a "heap big Injun" caddie does his stuff. This golf course has real Indian caddies. Also, the links is laid out on the site of an historic Chippewa Indian battlefield, with Indian mounds for bunkers, Indian spears to support the flags, Indian hammerheads and stone spears for tee markers, and wicker benches at the tees.

I don't think we'll ever know if this was an accurate account, or a story concocted by a writer at *Captain Billy's Whiz Bang* magazine. We do have a story about the early caddy days at Breezy Point that Lynn Headlee of Pequot Lakes recounted in the Breezy Pointer newsletter in 2007. Headlee remembered hitching a ride on the six-mile dirt road between Pequot Lakes and Breezy Point in 1928 so he could caddy at the golf course. Caddies earned 40 cents for nine holes and 75 cents for eighteen. Tips were few and there could be as many as 20 boys waiting for jobs sometimes. During the Prohibition Era, some of the golf bags might be a little heavier than usual. Lynn said, "Some guests came to play a round (golf) and others came to play around!" He caddied for many celebrities at Breezy, including golfer Patty Berg. Billy Fawcett wanted to have all the amenities available for his guests and took care of his caddies. He often bought ice cream for the group and once settled a strike for more pay. Caddies would now earn 50 cents for nine holes!

Breezy Point Caddies from the 1930s (L-R) Denny Gustafson, Jim Brunes, Ivor Knudson, Lynn Headlee, George Keprios, Bud Keprios, and Jake Larson at a 1982 Breezy Point reunion

Breezy Point general manager Dave Gravdahl also remembers getting his start as a caddie at the golf course in 1953. Gravdahl recalls hitching a ride with his friend Jack Schmidt to get from

Pequot Lakes to the golf course. Dave said the old nine-hole course was laid out so the golfers would come back to the club-house every three holes in case they needed to pick up a drink. Sometimes they would even buy a pop for the caddies! Schmidt began his caddie career in 1949 as a 12-year-old hitchhiking a newly paved road from Pequot to Breezy. Jack made $185 that summer and remembers picking out his school clothes from a Montgomery Ward catalog and paying for them with part of his summer earnings.

Caddies Eddie Nickel, Jimmy Nickel, and Mike Greer watch their golfers tee off during the Paul Bunyan Sports Club tournament at Breezy in 1953. The bag is almost as tall as Eddie!

Besides caddying, boys could make money hawking golf balls and selling them. The right side of hole 6 had a steep, brush-covered slope on the right side full of poison ivy. Golfers would hit their ball in there and tell the caddies not to bother looking for it because of all the poison ivy, but the caddies would return after the round and search for golf balls there. Titleist Acushnet's and Wilson K-28s were the prized balls and would fetch a quarter in the pro shop or 50 cents if the caddie sold it to a golfer himself. Schmidt caddied for some of the University of Minnesota coaches and former athletes who played quite frequently at the Breezy Point course during the Paul Bunyan Sports Club tournament. The best golfer Jack ever caddied for was an Illinois amateur champion named Bob Baker, who would drive up to the course in a white 1951 Oldsmobile convertible with red leather interior. Baker played matches at Breezy with other players, sometimes for up to $50 a hole. Big money in those days. Caddies carried the golf bag, cleaned the clubs and golf balls, replaced divots, raked the sand traps, gave their player the correct distance and line for each shot, and kept an eye on their player's ball so it wouldn't get lost.

The picture above, taken in 1954, shows the old clubhouse at Breezy Point that was built in 1935. Breezy had an active caddie program, but all four golfers in the picture were using pushcarts or trolleys to make their way around the golf course. Pushcarts became popular after World War II and were used by many golfers until motorized golf carts took over. Jack Schmitt called them "iron monsters," as they usually meant there was no need for a caddie.

The picture below, taken in 1957, shows one of the first motorized golf carts in use at Breezy Point. Golf carts had been around since the 1930s but became popular in the mid to late 1950s. It was the beginning of the end for caddies at Breezy Point.

Originally, golf carts were available at golf courses only for people who were unable to walk the course. Some courses would require a note from a doctor before allowing a golfer to ride. Once courses realized the amount of income cart rentals could provide, it then became the wave of the future. Today's golf carts have replaced the caddie with GPS systems that show a picture of the hole you're playing, with the yardage from your ball to the pin on the green. Carts can have a ball washer and club cleaner attached, and a sand bottle on board to help the player fill in their divots. Almost everything a caddie used to do is now provided by a golf cart. Breezy Point's three golf courses have more than 180 golf carts available, which are included in the price of your green fee.

One of Breezy Point's local golf carts. Some of them are pretty fancy!

In addition, many of the members at the Whitebirch and Traditional golf courses own their own golf carts and use them when playing golf. One of the first golfers to have their own cart at Breezy Point was club champion Don Heidt. Heidt liked to play a lot of golf, and he liked to play fast. His cart helped him move around the course quickly. When playing against Don in the 1970 Billy Fawcett tournament, I remember walking and carrying my bag while Don drove his three-wheeled Harley Davidson cart alongside me. The city of Breezy Point has allowed licensed and registered golf carts to drive on the city streets for over 25 years now. They currently have 649 carts licensed to travel in the city limits. With the current population listed at 2,429 people and at least two people in most families, one could assume about half of the families in Breezy Point now have a golf cart licensed to travel in town.

"Golf cannot be a complete journey unless you have someone at your side." –Ben Crenshaw

By replacing the caddie with a golf cart, golfers do lose out on one thing. The caddie was another person with a vested interest in a golfer's play and was there to both cheer for the good shots and offer encouragement when things weren't going well. A golf cart will never be able to do that. When I played in the Resorters Golf Tournament in 1988, my nine-year-old son Marcus was my caddie. Playing against one of the local favorites in a semifinal match, I noticed close to a hundred people following us. Everyone was rooting for my opponent, except for my caddie and me. With our match tied on the 18th hole, my opponent hit his approach to 15 feet while I missed the green and left my ball down a steep bank left of the green. As we walked toward the green, I remember Marcus telling me how well I had played that week. With tears coming out of his eyes, he told me that he was proud of me. I looked at him with a smile and said, "Marcus, the match isn't over yet." I pitched my ball a foot from the hole to make par and tie the hole, then hit another good chip shot close on the first playoff hole, securing the win. You don't get that kind of interaction or inspiration from a golf cart!

Youngsters don't have a chance to caddie much anymore, but they can find other ways to spend a summer working at the golf course. Courses continue to employ kids to load clubs onto carts, clean the carts and clubs at the end of the round, and set up and pick up practice balls on the driving range. Instead of caddies, they're now outside service workers. They no longer need to hitch-hike to work. Most drive their own vehicle. Like the caddie, they receive wages and tips, and all of them make more money in one week than caddie Jack Schmidt made the entire summer of 1949.

Chapter 6: The Times They Are A-Changin'

In 1963, Robert Zimmerman of Hibbing (a city 80 miles northwest of Breezy Point) was writing a song that would become the anthem of the 1960s. Now going by the name Bob Dylan, the former University of Minnesota student declared to the world in three minutes and fifteen seconds of music that "The Times They Are A-Changin'"—and change they did. It was the age of Aquarius, when Jupiter aligned with Mars. But peace would not guide the planet this decade. Hair got longer, music got louder, and a fight for freedom and equality took over as civil rights, women's rights, and the anti-war movement swept the country. Many would lose their lives, including politicians like the Kennedy brothers, civil rights leaders like Martin Luther King Jr., soldiers in Vietnam, and even students, like the four at Kent State University shot by the Ohio National Guard in 1970.

Times were changing at Breezy Point as well, as the resort attempted to recover from the fire that destroyed the lodge in 1959. Current owners were the Bremor Corporation, an amalgamation of Jack Salenger and friends from Chicago, with Ken Kellar running the resort as an agent for the corporation. Bremor was not paying any interest payments on their loan, no taxes were being paid, and resort workers were having trouble getting paid for their work. Still holding onto the contract for deed, Brownie Cote decided to repossess the resort in July of 1960 to protect his interest in the Breezy Point operation. The resort was closed for part of the summer while the question of ownership dragged through the courts. The golf course remained open, and the Ten Thousand Lakes Tournament was held with defending champion Len Bjorklund winning again. Cote took over ownership of Breezy Point in 1961 and mapped out a building plan that included an addition to the dining room and convention hall area that provided space for 1,000 people. The golf course was closed for a good part of the season, and no tournament was held. The newly formed Minnesota Vikings football team received an offer to hold their pre-season training camp at the resort.

When jobs were scarce during the Great Depression of the 1930s, Captain Billy Fawcett would offer summer employment to University of Minnesota athletes for $100 a month plus room and board. This 1939 photo shows five Gophers football players taking time out from their jobs to get in some conditioning on the beach at Pelican Lake. In the back row are halfbacks Chuck Myre and Leland Johnson, with Helge Pukema, Bob Green, and John Mariucci lining up in front. They also played golf throughout the summer to stay in shape for football. When Walter Hagen and John Montague played their exhibition match at Breezy in July, Myre and Mariucci were recruited as caddies for the two pros.

In a scene straight out of the old Billy Fawcett days, football was looking to return to Breezy Point in 1961. A March 22 article in the *Brainerd Dispatch* indicated the Minnesota Vikings were giving strong consideration to hosting their very first training camp at Breezy Point Resort. The offer from Breezy Point included complete control of the lodge for the full 45-day training period. The 370-acre resort had 45 cottages and 12 other rooms, 1,500 feet of sand beach, many miles of wooded trails, a marina, two swimming pools, tennis courts, a complete golf fairway to be used as two practice fields, and three shower rooms—with an offer to remodel the latter if required.

Lodge owner Brownie Cote backed up the offer with an extremely low daily cost per man in his bid. The Vikings would bring 85 of their own people plus another 15 or more in a press contingent. The actual training period would cover 36 days, but the group would stay 45 days, giving great publicity to the area during their stay.

As it turned out, Bemidji State University had better facilities to offer and was selected over Breezy Point for the site of the Vikings' first training camp. Breezy then offered their facilities to the Dallas Cowboys but did not get that bid either as the Cowboys decided to train at St. Olaf College in Northfield, Minnesota. No football cleats would touch the fairways at Breezy Point that year, only spikes from golf shoes.

The Vikings delegation, including owner Ole Haugsrud, general manager Bert Rose, and head coach Norm Van Brocklin, checked out the first hole at Breezy Point's golf course. Training camp plans would include two practice football fields being placed on the fairway of the 330-yard hole.

Rose and Van Brocklin, who impressed everyone he met with his ready smile and gracious manner, check out photos of boxer Jack Dempsey and Notre Dame football coach Knut Rockne at the Breezy Point Lodge. Dempsey and Rockne were friends and guests of Captain Fawcett at Breezy Point.

By 1962, the resort was up and running again with Cote in charge. In a move to bring back the good old days of Billy Fawcett, big name bands like the Count Basie, Glenn Miller, and Tommy Dorsey orchestras were brought in to perform at Breezy Point during the summer.

Unlike the exclusiveness of the Fawcett era, Cote planned to make the resort a public playground as well as an entertainment center for the area with all of the resort facilities open to the public on a fee basis.

In addition, 200 lots were plotted out for sale on land adjacent to Pelican Lake and the Breezy Point golf course. This included the old McIntyre land holding Billy Fawcett had purchased in 1926 with plans to add a second nine to the golf course.

By the end of the 1962 season, Brownie Cote had enough of trying to run a second resort and wanted to focus his time on his Gull Lake resort, Grandview Lodge.

In January of 1963, he announced plans to sell Breezy Point to Don Eastvold and Ginny Simms of Palm Springs, California. A Minnesota native, Eastvold was a former attorney general for the state of Washington and Simms a big-band singer who also appeared in several Hollywood B-list movies. Recently married, the two were looking to branch out into real estate development. California cool was coming to Breezy Point with BIG changes in store!

In March, Don and Ginny revealed their plan to create Minnesota's first country club community. Their multimillion-dollar development would include a 2,600-foot blacktopped air strip, a 200-slip boat marina, weekly big name entertainment at the resort, and lakeshore condominiums.

Seven hundred homesite lots were plotted along the fairways of the golf course. A new clubhouse was built, and plans were made to expand the golf course to 18 holes. Construction of condominiums and new homes eliminated the signature par-3 seventh hole and changed the eighth hole from a par-5 to a shorter par-4.

The *Brainerd Dispatch* reported on April 4, 1964: "Bulldozers are at work in the area that was once the seventh hole of the nine-hole Breezy Point golf course. A 100-unit condominium is being constructed. An additional 10 holes have been added to the golf course."

Architect Bill Maurer of Palm Springs, California, added 10 holes across County Road 4 that were cut through a thick forest of Norway Pines. While not long, the holes were extremely tight and demanded accurate golf shots.

In addition, Maurer designed a 9-hole par-3 course along the lakeshore in front of the supper club, giving Breezy Point 27 holes of golf!

The par-3 course is no longer there, but the other 18 holes comprise today's Traditional Golf Course. Holes one, six, seven, eight, nine, 10, 17, and 18 remain from the original course. Holes two through five and 11 through 16 are part of the new Maurer design.

The eighth hole was originally a 492-yard par-5. New home construction in 1963 took over most of the area in this picture. The tee was moved up on top of the hill, making it a 352-yard par-4.

Courtesy of the Brainerd Dispatch, this picture shows construction of one of the new holes being cut through a thick forest of Norway pines in 1963.

Minnesota governor Karl Rolvaag, a college classmate of Don Eastvold, was on hand in June for the grand opening of Breezy Point Estates. Brownie Cote stayed on through the summer as the resident manager, and 12 full-time salesmen arrived from California to sell the new property. Dressed in California-cool gold chains and leisure suits, they used a high-pressure sales pitch to sell lots and fill spaces in the condominiums being built at a rapid pace.

With the change in ownership at Breezy in 1963, PGA pro Max Evans from Palm Springs, California, took over as head professional. Max had turned pro in 1946 after four years of military service. He was an assistant pro at Pine Lake in Michigan and played on the PGA Tour during the winter months. He played out of Sunnybrook GC, where he held the course record with a 28-33—61, and competed full-time on the PGA Tour throughout the 1950s. He was considered one of the longest drivers on tour and once held the PGA record at 327 yards, but a knee injury cut his tour career short.

The highlight of a somewhat undistinguished career was a victory at the 1955 Long Island Open. Evans closed with two rounds of 67-67 to edge out "terrible tempered" Tommy Bolt and a young up-and-comer named Arnold Palmer. He competed in the 1955 Masters, finishing 27th, and played in three U.S. Opens, with his best finish being 23rd place at Baltusrol in 1954.

Evans was also on hand at the Tucson Open in 1952, one of the few tournaments of that time that allowed African American golfers to play. Max's first-round 67 was two strokes ahead of heavyweight champion Joe Louis and three strokes in front of professional Ted Rhodes. Because the PGA Tour had a "caucasians only" clause at that time, most PGA events would not have allowed those two to play due to the color of their skin! Evans finished 15 strokes behind winner Henry Williams with a 289; Rhodes finished with 292; and Louis ended up withdrawing from the tournament.

The new clubhouse at Breezy Point, constructed in 1963

After retiring from the tour full-time, Evans held club jobs in Las Vegas and Palm Springs before coming to Breezy Point in 1963. Following his year at Breezy, Max returned to Michigan and continued to work as a pro, giving lessons at several courses and driving ranges in the Detroit area. In 2001, he received his 50-year membership pin from the PGA. At 81, he was still teaching people how to play golf.

This aerial photo from 1964 shows 10 new holes added across County Road 4.

Par-3 Course by the Lake

"There are no interesting approach and putt courses in America. A really good one requires as much thought and planning as a full course." –Alister MacKenzie, 1932

Short golf courses can trace their beginnings back to Scotland where the Wee Course at North Berwick dates back to 1888. In 1932, famed golf course architect Alister MacKenzie drew up a 9-hole short course to accompany the 18-hole Augusta National course he had just finished. Unfortunately, the onset of the Great Depression put those plans on hold. Twenty-five years later, Augusta chairman Clifford Roberts asked architect George Cobb to design a par-3 course for Augusta. The 1,060-yard layout opened in 1958, and the Masters' first Par 3 contest was held in 1960. It has been a tournament fixture for over 60 years. It's a festive occasion where family and friends are called on to caddie and sometimes hit a shot or two for their pro. Jack Nicklaus, winner of six green jackets, said his greatest day at Augusta was when caddie and grandson G. T. Nicklaus made a hole-in-one on the ninth hole during the Par 3 contest in 2018.

Captain Billy Fawcett and his wife visited the cradle of American golf in 1923 to see how a first-class golf resort operated. The original nine holes at Pinehurst were laid out in 1898. Today, that same land is the site of a par-3 course known as "the Cradle." Designed by Gil Hanse in 2017, the Cradle is 789 yards of fun that can be enjoyed by golfers of all ages and skill levels. Music is piped in through speakers hidden throughout the course. The signature third hole has a punchbowl green with elevated Adirondack chairs on the surrounding hill where spectators can sit, have a beverage, and cheer on shots coming into the green.

The past decade has seen a rise in shorter courses all across the country. Needing less room, they are cheaper to build. Owners can charge people less to play, and golfers can get around the course in much less time than a regular golf course requires. It's a win-win for everyone. Par-3 courses have now made their way into the Brainerd Lakes area. Scott Hoffman Design created the Gravel Pit in 2021. Located just north of Cragun's Legacy courses, the Gravel Pit is a 13-hole par-3 design. With an accompanying putting course, bocce ball court, and driving range, it is a family event center where everyone can participate and have fun.

Gravel Pit Golf Course in Brainerd, MN

When it comes to par-3 courses in this area, Breezy Point was 60 years ahead of its time. Architect Bill Mauer was hired in 1963 to design a second nine holes at Breezy Point that would allow for home site development around the Traditional Golf Course. In addition to the main course, he also built a short par-3 pitch and putt course on the point of land separating Breezy Point Bay from Big

Pelican Lake. Located directly in front of the Supper Club, the par-3 course traveled along the lakeshore, with a few holes playing across some of the water. The 535-yard design was the ideal playground for young and old alike. Greg Johnson has shot 64 at both the Traditional and Whitebirch golf courses. He remembers summers at Breezy where he would go around and around the par-3 course for days at a time. "As a toddler, this course was my playpen," Johnson told me. Peter Hoffman recalls sneaking on the course at night and playing by the lights from the resort until Charlie Paige arrived to chase him away. Five-time Orv's Invitational champion Joe Towle also grew up at Breezy playing the par-3 course.

Towle recalled, "We stayed at the beachside condos right next door, so the par-3 was part of our regular routine. I played it hundreds of times in the 1970s." Joe was kind enough to find a postcard picture of the resort from the 1960s and map out the par-3 layout on it. Distances are approximate for each par-3 hole:

Hole 1: 80 yards   Hole 2: 40 yards   Hole 3: 50 yards
Hole 4: 70 yards   Hole 5: 90 yards   Hole 6: 40 yards
Hole 7: 30 yards   Hole 8: 70 yards   Hole 9: 65 yards

Par 3 Hole Layout

William H. Maurer: Traditional Golf Course Architect

The Fawcett family sold the Breezy Point Resort after World War II. It went through several owners over the next two decades until it was purchased by Don Eastvold and Ginny Simms in 1963. Eastvold and Simms had big plans for the resort that included an expansion of the golf course. They hired a 25-year-old former golf pro turned land developer, William H. Maurer of Palm Springs, to lay out the new holes, with homesites plotted alongside each of the holes. Maurer designed a short par-3 course down by Pelican Lake and added 10 new holes to the west of the original course. One of the original holes was replaced by a motel, thus the need for 10 new holes to make up an 18-hole course. Bill Maurer also served as general manager at the resort for a short time before moving on.

PLANNING FOR YOUR PLEASURE

Project manager Jerry Lenz, restaurant manager Mario Vaccarino, general resort manager Bill Maurer, and sales manager Buzz Prince go over Breezy Point plans in 1963.

Maurer went on to form Diamondhead Corporation and continued to plant golf course communities in parts of Oklahoma, Texas, and Mississippi. Each development featured a golf course surrounded by homesites, promises of the many amenities that would be available if you purchased a homesite, and a high-pressure sales staff eager to close on the sale of each lot. Some of these developments were successful, but many had trouble getting off the ground, mostly because of a lack of money from sales.

In partnership with a wealthy businessman named Malcolm McLean, Maurer and Diamondhead purchased the Pinehurst Resort and approximately 7,500 acres of land from the Tufts family (the original resort owners) in 1971 for $9.2 million. The company laid out 6,000 single-family lots on a portion of that land. Anyone who purchased a lot was promised use of the golf courses and other recreational facilities at Pinehurst. To the dismay of Pinehurst residents, Diamondhead also began to line the fairways of courses 3 and 5 with condominiums.

Maurer came to Pinehurst with some big ideas. Golf was one sport that had never established a hall of fame. Bill thought Pinehurst, the home of American golf, was the ideal location for one.

He built a $2.5-million facility next to Pinehurst No. 2 and established the World Golf Hall of Fame there in 1974. President Gerald Ford spoke at the opening ceremony, and three golfers with ties to Breezy Point—Walter Hagen, Patty Berg, and Arnold Palmer—were among the original hall of fame members.

Pinehurst had not hosted a professional golf tournament since 1951. Maurer decided to bring the pros back to Pinehurst in 1973 for a two-week, 144-hole World Golf Hall of Fame Classic, which gave out a check for $100,000 to the winner. 144 holes proved to be too much golf, so the tournament went back to 72 holes the next year until it ended in 1982. Bill Maurer's tenure at Pinehurst did not last as long as his golf tournament. Like a supernova, his flame burned bright at first, fueled by big plans and ideas, but just as quickly, he began to burn out until he was no longer around. In November of 1974, shortly after the World Golf Hall of Fame opened, he was relieved of his duties as president of Diamondhead. Using their profits from Pinehurst, Diamondhead had plans for other residential golf course developments in Alabama and Georgia. To buy time for their other projects to succeed, they mortgaged their Pinehurst holdings to the banks. By the end of 1981, overextended and out of money, they could no longer meet their payment to the banks. Diamondhead's reign in Pinehurst was over. The World Golf Hall of Fame left Pinehurst and relocated to the World Golf Village near St. Augustine, Florida, in 1998.

To borrow from the poet Dylan Thomas, Bill Maurer did not

"go gently into that good night." A large man, Bill was the prover-bial bull in a china closet. Every time he moved, it seemed some-thing would break. A tireless self-promoter, he had plaques made for $10,000 each in 1974 for the original Golf Hall of Fame mem-bers as well as one for himself as its "founder." That did not sit well with a great many people. Hall of Fame president Don Collett said, "Bill got things done, but he had a knack for rubbing people the wrong way. If he had a main fault, it was that he tried to do too much, too soon." Maurer found his way back to Palm Springs, Cal-ifornia, where he was pictured on the cover of *Palm Springs Life* magazine in June of 1976. Together with Johnny Dawson, they created a new golf club design that was marketed as the "Unique golf iron." Dawson was a fine amateur golfer who worked for Spal-ding Golf for a number of years before creating the Thunderbird and Eldorado country clubs in Palm Springs. He and Maurer were friends from the 1950s when Bill worked as a teaching pro at In-dian Wells Country Club. Their patented iron design featured a thick-rounded bottom surface to help get the ball airborne. The cavity-backed club was similar to the Spalding Executive iron, which came out around 1977. After developing and starting pro-duction on the golf club, Maurer sold his interest in the company to the E. F. MacDonald Co. in July of 1980. Unique Golf went out of business shortly after that.

Now settled in the Palm Springs area, Maurer created several startup companies over the next two decades, including the San Carlos Development Corporation (1982), W.H. Maurer LTD (1983), Home Utilities Savers of Houston (1985), International Re-sort Properties (1989), AMPRO International Golf Tour (1995 pa-tent), and the Esterus Swing Institute (2001) in Palm Desert, which offered golf instruction. Nothing would come of any of these ven-tures, and Bill eventually faded off into the sunset. I'm sure he would be happy to know that Breezy Point is now a golf destination enjoyed by golfers from across the United States and Canada and that the World Golf Hall of Fame is relocating back to Pinehurst in 2024, where the USGA will once again play two U.S. Opens back-to-back in 2028. That will be 144 holes of golf in two weeks. I wonder who thought of that?

Bill Maurer left Breezy Point just in time. By 1965, rumors were rife about Breezy Point being unable to pay their bills. Several companies took the resort to court in an effort to collect what they were owed. Russ and Patty Carlyle were entertainers at the resort during this time. Patty remembers getting golf clubs and golf lessons in lieu of cash several times when Breezy was unable to pay the musicians. When moving vans arrived near the end of the summer to clear things out, she recalled seeing money taped to the walls of some of the trucks. Like Billy Fawcett, Eastvold and Simms had come to Breezy Point with lots of big ideas and plans. They tried to do too much too soon and unfortunately did not have Captain Billy's deep pockets to pay for their ticket. Over 250 creditors presented claims against the resort estimated at over $3 million. Breezy Point filed for bankruptcy in the fall, and the creditors lined up to get what they could.

Golf went on through all the turmoil. The new back-9 officially opened in July, and the annual golf tournament was finally played on an 18-hole golf course. Many of the state's top golfers were on hand, but the man everyone came to see was a famous golf hustler from Chicago, Kenny Pinns. Pinns had just won the top three summer resort tournaments in Minnesota and would try to capture the Breezy Point tournament to give him a "Minnesota Slam." There had to be some money involved, as Pinns only played golf when there was something on the line to play for.

The Minnesota summer resort golf tournaments attracted

golfers and fans from across the country. Minnesota summers by the lake offered people from Texas, Oklahoma, Kansas, Nebraska, and other places a chance to escape the summer heat. Their interest in golf, along with a large amount of expendable income, made the resort tournaments famous for the size of their betting pool, which was called the Calcutta. After the qualifying rounds were concluded, people would gather for the auction. Bids were placed according to the confidence the group had in the player's ability to advance in the tournament. Typically, the winner's share of the Calcutta pool was around 40%, with smaller shares paid out for second-place, semi-final, and quarterfinal competitors. Every player had someone rooting for them to play well.

I never paid much attention to the Calcutta when I played, as it was one more thing to occupy a mind that needed to be focused on golf. It wasn't too hard to figure out who might have put some money on you, though. Playing in my club championship one year, I noticed my friend and former Breezy Point competitor Joe Ryan in the gallery, keeping an eye on every shot. Since I had won the tournament several times, I was one of the favorites and probably went for quite a bit of money in the Calcutta. Playing the last hole with a sizeable lead, I walked over to Joe and joked that, in honor of my dad, I was going to play my chip shot just short of the green with his favorite club, an eight-iron. Joe looked at me in all seriousness and said, "You have an uphill lie. Maybe you should use a 7-iron instead." I was already celebrating, but the Calcutta money was still grinding away!

At the other end of the spectrum, in my first year at the Resorters tournament, I qualified for the Executive Championship and played my way into the finals against my friend George Cliff. As a newcomer, I was probably a cheap buy at the pre-tournament Calcutta. Right before George and I teed off in the championship match, a gentleman who played with us in the qualifying round walked over. With a drink in each hand, Al put his arms around both of us and said, "All I can say, gentlemen, is may the best man win, because I bought both of you at the Calcutta. If you'll excuse me, I'm going to go to the pro shop now and order myself a new set of golf clubs!"

Kenny Pinns was a man who played golf for a living. He wasn't a professional golfer. Ken made his living hustling and gambling. He lived in a time when big-money games were set up between good players, gamblers, and fools with big egos. When the golf game was over, there was always a card game or a dice game going on, and Kenny excelled at all of them. He was also a tremendous pool player. Many times, in a game of 9-ball, Pinns would run the table and collect his winnings without giving his opponent a chance to take a shot!

Standing 6'3" with broad shoulders and long black hair combed straight back, he looked like a tough competitor. Kenny was a good athlete who had played AAU basketball back in the 1940s with NBA hall of famer George Mikan before turning to golf in the 1950s. He tied for 15th place behind champion Doug Sanders in the amateur division of the Tam O'Shanter tournament in Chicago in 1955. Patty Berg received a $1,000 check for winning the ladies division of the tournament, and Doug Ford captured the top professional spot and $3,240. Pinns tried his luck on the PGA Tour without much success from 1957-60 before applying to be reinstated as an amateur. He did qualify for the U.S. Open in 1958 but missed the cut.

In 1962, as a reinstated amateur, Ken teamed up with fellow Tam O'Shanter golfer and notorious gambler Martin Stanovich (AKA the "Fat Man") to travel the country playing big-time tournaments and big-money matches. In April, they teamed up at the

International Four-Ball in Miami, shooting four rounds in the 60s to finish second to two teenage phenoms from South Florida. June of 1962 saw the two men cross the Atlantic Ocean to compete in the French and British amateur tournaments. The Fat Man lost his first-round match in France while Pinns lost by default, so it was on to England and the 100th playing of the British Amateur at Hoylake. The weather was terrible all week. The golfers dreaded trifecta of cold, wind, and rain, which might explain Kenny defaulting again. Stanovich, however, made it to the third round before an "injury" to his right arm caused him to lose that match. Better weather later in the summer saw Pinns qualify for the U.S. Amateur at Pinehurst No. 2 and make it to the second round before losing.

July found the two golfers in Bemidji, Minnesota, for the 1962 Birchmont International. After the first round of qualifying, they sat in second and third place with a 2-under 70 (Pinns) and a 1-under 71 (Stanovich). Since the lowest qualifiers usually go for the most money at the Calcutta auction, the two men shot significantly higher scores in the second round to move back in the pack a bit and lower their price at the auction that night. By the luck of the draw, the two friends played each other in the quarterfinal round. Playing under-par golf as he had in every match that week, Ken prevailed 1-up and then went on to poke in a four-foot birdie putt on the 18th green that Sunday to defeat Bill Larson 1-up in the finals. The new champion was four under par on the last day! Pinns and the Fat Man also played in the two remaining resort tournaments that summer, which served as a prelude to his magical season three years later.

In 1965, a Minneapolis "businessman" ostensibly hired Kenny to play in and win the three resort tournaments in Northern Minnesota: the Birchmont in Bemidji, the Resorters in Alexandria, and the Pine to Palm in Detroit Lakes. Played over three consecutive weeks in late July and early August, the resort tournaments attracted great players, many of who later went on to play the PGA Tour. In 1965 alone, there were four competitors in the three events who eventually qualified for and played on the PGA Tour. Rumor has it that Pinns was paid $1,000 a week to play in and win the three tournaments. Amazingly, he did just that, the only time anyone has accomplished that feat. Ken played 52-under-par golf for the 357 holes it took him to win 16 matches in a row over a three-week period. The Calcutta pools at these tournaments were at their peak. In 1965, they were probably in excess of $100,000 for the three tournaments with the winner's share of 40% going to Pinns' backer—more than $40,000. To put that in perspective, it would be the equivalent of $330,000 in today's money! According to my friend John Lieser, the winner would usually get a percentage of the winnings as well. As John tells it, after winning the Pine to Palm title in 1971, "Shadow surreptitiously shoved a check into my pocket, as it was customary to give the winner 10%." Along with his weekly stipend, that would bring Ken's three-week share to over $7,000—or $58,000 in today's money!

Playing out of Las Vegas, Nevada, in 1965, Kenny Pinns started out slowly at the Birchmont but progressively got better and better each day. He birdied the first three holes in his final match against Texan Keith Jorde on his way to a 5 & 4 victory. He continued his hot hand at the Resorters, where he was medalist with a 6 under par 138 (66-72). Pinns was 21 under par on his way to the finals. His quarterfinal opponent, John Lieser, described it this way after losing 6 & 5: "Pinns was the consummate shot-maker who rose to the occasion when he needed to—he seemed to toy with me. I was impressed with his cool demeanor, and it seemed he had lots of game in reserve, and when presented, he could produce whatever shot was needed." That was evident in his final match against defending champion Neil Croonquist. Pinns boomed his tee shot 30 yards short of the green on the 340-yard 18th hole. This was back in the days of balata balls and wooden drivers! He chipped up five feet short of the cup from there and gently curled the birdie putt in to win the match 1-up. It was his only close match all week as he finished a total of 23 under par for the week! Afterward, he told a reporter, "I'm a little golfed out right now and I'm really not sure if I'll play at Detroit Lakes. But if I can get a ride up there, I'd like to take a look at the course."

He found a ride courtesy of fellow competitor Dick Blooston as he easily qualified for the championship and put on another birdie barrage on his way to the finals. In his opening round match, he made five straight birdies on holes 3-7 at the Detroit Lakes course. His semifinal opponent was medalist Bob Dahm. Pinns had narrowly escaped Dahm 1-up in the Birchmont semis. He crushed Dahm this time, winning the first eight holes with a string of birdies en route to an 8 & 7 victory! Once again, he made a short birdie putt on the 18th green to cap off a 2-up decision over defending champion Dave Hanten in the final match, 52 under par for 357 holes. It was a three-week stretch of golf never seen before or since in Minnesota.

After taking a couple of weeks off to recuperate, Pinns sent his entry in for the Breezy Point Invitational. Formerly the Ten Thousand Lakes Championship, this tournament was one of the original resort tournaments back in the 1920s and 1930s. It had always attracted a strong field of Minnesota's best golfers. With the change of ownership at Breezy Point, the tournament had gone through its own changes. Normally played in early July, the Breezy tournament was now scheduled over Labor Day weekend. A match play tournament in its heyday, this year it was one day of qualifying followed by 36 holes of medal play. The Calcutta was still around, though, which would explain Ken's interest in playing here.

Chuck Chalberg of Brainerd and Cos Egan of Interlachen led the qualifying round with 68s. Kenny shot a 71, and defending champion John Taylor shot 72. Rain on Saturday washed out the opening round and would reduce the tournament to 27 holes on Sunday. Don Peddie remembers Pinns going out to hit a few wedge shots south of the first tee during the rain. Returning to the clubhouse, he gave a short class on how to operate pari-mutuel betting, or what might be called a horse race, paying out for win, place, and show. The championship round on Sunday did not play out without a controversy. After 18 holes, Pinns had a 69 to hold a one-shot lead over Chalberg at 70, and two shots over Egan at 71. The rain continued to fall, and the golf course was saturated. There was talk of stopping play and making it an 18-hole tournament. Chalberg remembers that Dr. Bob Harris, the all-state defenseman on the 1946 state championship Roseau hockey team, was the only one who spoke up to keep playing. Chuck recalls Harris insisting, "This isn't fair. Let's keep playing. Give the kid a chance to beat him!" It wasn't to be. The course was wet, and everyone wanted to go home. Game over. Pinns wins again.

Minneapolis Star-Tribune golf writer Dwayne Netland summed the 1965 Minnesota golf season up best in a December 28, 1965, column titled "Golfer Of The Year: The Hustler":

"...there has to be some post-season recognition for what Kenny Pinns did on the resort trail last summer. Regardless of whether or not you admire his instincts for the wager, you've got to admit he provided a lot of color for the tourists who follow these tournaments. Here he comes now, striding up the fairway, his dark hair slicked down, his tanned face furrowed in concentration. With him were half a dozen colleagues from who knows where, their wallets riding on every shot. Kenny had the shots, all of them. There was never really much doubt over the outcome of his matches. He is a foot-loose man, and we may never see him again. But it was fun to have him around."

And finally this, from Kenny's good friend Dave Rovick: "All you have to say about Kenny Pinns' game is that the ball was always going toward the hole."

In addition to Pinns, the 1965 tournament featured one of Minnesota's top female golfers. After shooting a 74 in her qualifying round, Bev Vanstrom was asked if she would like to play in the men's division instead. She declined the invitation. Bev won the women's title, defeating Duluth's Cleo Burton with a rain-shortened nine-hole score of 40. A member of the Minnesota Golf Hall of Fame, Mrs. Vanstrom was the state women's amateur champion in 1954, 1955, 1957, and 1962. She also won seven MWGA match play titles and six MWGA stroke play titles for a career record total of 17 major state women's golf championships. Bev also has two Birchmont titles and one Resorters crown to go along with her Breezy Point championship.

With the resort in bankruptcy, Minneapolis businessman Lloyd Brandvold leased the resort for two years from 1966 to 1967. Billy Fawcett's youngest son, Roscoe, came to the rescue and sponsored the annual golf tournament. Renamed the Billy Fawcett Memorial Golf Tournament, Roscoe provided the impressive Roscoe Fawcett trophy for the champion each year.

Long rumored to be interested in acquiring the resort, Minneapolis-based Hopkins House purchased Breezy Point in 1968. They kept nine holes open on the east side of the golf course while the maintenance crew worked on restoring the new holes, which had been dormant for a while and were overgrown with weeds. By the end of the 1968 season, all 18 holes were back in play. Along with the par three course, this gave Breezy Point's customers 27 holes of golf. As the 1960s drew to a close, Breezy Point finally had some stable ownership to start the long process of building the resort back up again.

Left: Kenny Pinns, far right, celebrates another victory! Below: 1965 women's champion Bev Vanstrom (from the book Minnesota Golf: 90 Years of Tournament History)

1967 champion Art Hayes and 1966 champion Don Peddie pose with the Roscoe Fawcett trophy

Chapter 7: The Decade of Disruption

The Beatles break up, a sitting president resigns amid scandal, the Vietnam War ends, and the pet rock arrives. And that's just the beginning of the 1970s. Innovative inventions from this time are still felt today whenever one writes a reminder on a Post-it note or heats up food in a microwave oven—at our house, it's known as the "popcorn popper." New lines of communication were opened up with the invention of the mobile phone, Apple computers arrived in 1977 along with floppy disc storage, the Sony Walkman enabled music to be portable, and video games could now be played on your TV screen. Finally, after years of economic growth, our country found itself locked in a new recession called "stagflation," a combination of high unemployment and high interest rates. It became worse in 1973 when the Middle East oil countries declared an embargo against the United States in response to our support of Israel. Long lines formed at gas stations as Americans struggled to put gas in their cars at a much higher price. Stagflation would slow growth in the country to a near standstill for much of the decade.

Not good news for the new owners trying to revive a struggling resort. High gas prices made it harder for people to travel, and high interest rates made it difficult for new development to start up.

Hopkins House had to take a slower approach to building up Breezy Point. In 1974, the new owners, together with Don Eastvold's former partner Jerry Lenz, took the plunge and purchased 2,300 acres of land to the west of the resort. Planning for a new development—called Whitebirch, Inc.—included three main components: a camping and condominium community, an 18-hole championship golf course, and estate lot development. Plans were for more than 40% of the area to remain open or "green" space, with trails for cross-country skiing, hiking, cycling, snowmobiling, and horseback riding. According to Breezy Point general manager Jim Harmon, "A new golf course is a must as the present 18-hole course has become overcrowded during the peak season. Our new course will be the first championship-level golf course in this area." Harmon estimated the Whitebirch project would take three to four years to complete. Concerns from the local community and a stagnant economy would drag things out for a few more years. An Environmental Impact Statement for Whitebirch was approved in 1976, allowing development to begin on the first cluster of 300 campsites. Further development would have to wait for completion of the city's central sewage system. By 1977, the engineering consultant and planner for Whitebirch, Dexter Hubbard of Fredricksburg, Virginia, began surveying and staking the new golf course with the assistance of local resident Myron "Mike" Landecker. An avid golfer who served on the board of directors at Fredricksburg Country Club, Hubbard held a master's degree in engineering from Virginia Polytechnic Institute. That same year, investors brought in Jerry Lenz's friend Bob Spizzo to give their project a jump start. Whitebirch Campground was created, and soon work would begin on the new 18-hole championship golf course.

Hopkins House was able to bring some much-needed stability

to the resort in the 1970s. The golf course was featured in an article by golf writer Ralph Thornton of the *Minneapolis Star* in July of 1973. Thornton praised Breezy Point for setting a relaxed, easy pace that vacationers could all enjoy.

Breezy Sets Relaxed Pace

(June 30, 1973, article in the *Minneapolis Star* by golf writer Ralph Thornton)

Resort golf in Minnesota, though limited, offers the average golfer a chance to try interesting courses in a vacation atmosphere, as one Twin Cities quartet found out this week at Breezy Point near Pequot Lakes, Minn. "It's a good change from city courses," said Tom Coplin, St. Paul. "You don't feel pushed, you can relax and enjoy the game. You're almost alone on some holes." Coplin, his wife Jacque (pronounced Jackie), with Roger and Vicky Woitas of St. Paul, were at Breezy on a four-day Golf Holiday package costing each couple $59.95 for four days and three nights at the resort. "I made out on golf balls alone," noted Woitas, showing a bag of 30 he found in the woods bordering much of the course. The foursome played daily, sometimes two rounds totaling 36 holes.

One of the oldest resort courses in Minnesota, Breezy Point is short but sporty. The original nine holes were installed in 1924 by the late Wilford H. (Captain Billy) Fawcett, who made a fortune in magazine publications. Fawcett spent $250,000 on the golf course and surrounding camp for the entertainment of his friends, including movie stars and other celebrities. About 10 years ago, under the ownership of Don Eastvold and Ginny Simms another nine holes were built, with adjoining property earmarked for building sites. Therefore, much of the second nine has woods and out-of-bounds on both sides of the fairway.

"Never played here before? Better take lots of balls," warned a golfer on the tenth tee. "And use an iron off the tee." The advice was good- irons kept ball loss down, though on some holes were insufficient to reach the sharp doglegs to see the green for a second shot. Greens were excellent, well-watered and holding wedge shots well. Fairways were somewhat dry, but the growing season in Northern Minnesota is young and they should improve. Winter rules prevail through the summer. "I'd expected something better manicured," said Mrs. Coplin, who is handicap chairperson of the Ladies League at Brightwood Hills, New Brighton, where Mrs. Woitas is also a member. "But the people make up for it- everyone is courteous, and playing leisurely, no pressure."

Breezy Point's annual tournament, held over Labor Day weekend, has become an institution. Its defending champion? "Me, I guess," admitted course manager and two handicapper Doug Nelson, North Branch. "I've won it the past two years- I guess that's how I got this job." Nelson, 24, was a member of the North Branch high school golf team that won three consecutive state titles and later was NIC conference champion while attending St. Cloud State College.

Few resorts provide the ambience and leisurely enjoyment of half-century-old Breezy Point, now owned by the Hopkins House organization and still going strong. To the city golfer its pine-scented woods were a magnet to attract the golfer and his tee shot alike. FACILITIES AND FEES: 150 miles from Twin Cities near Pequot Lakes. Length 5,463 yards, par 68. Additional par 3 course.

Green fees are $5.75 for all day and $3 after 4:30. Reservations taken and necessary weekends.

The Billy Fawcett Tournament

In 1967, the Ten Thousand Lakes Tournament had its name changed to the Billy Fawcett Memorial Golf Tournament in honor of the founder of Breezy Point. Captain Billy's youngest son, Roscoe Kent Fawcett, served as honorary chairman and provided a rather expensive trophy each year for the tournament champion.

In 1970, there was a large group of junior golfers on hand for the Billy Fawcett Tournament. Dave McClellan of Tracy, Minnesota, was the medalist with a 4-over-par 72, while Daryl Ahlgren of Robbinsdale finished second with a 73.

McClellan lost his first-round match to Crosby-Ironton High School golfer Rich Aulie, 2-up. Defending champion Don Heidt made his way to the finals for a second time, where he faced Aulie, a 17-year-old high school senior.

With their match all even after the 11th hole, Rich drove it in the middle of the fairway at 12 while Heidt hooked his ball into the woods and had to chip it back to the fairway.

Aulie was not able to locate his ball in the fairway until a spectator noticed a small depression in the fairway covered over with grass the mower could not reach.

There was his ball, in the middle of the fairway and covered by grass four inches high! After being denied relief, Rich hacked the ball out and played his next shot to the green. Both golfers had short putts for bogeys, and Aulie holed his from 10 feet to win the hole.

He went on to win three of the next four holes to claim a 4 & 2 victory and the Billy Fawcett championship. Rich came back to Breezy Point in 1999, where he has worked as a player assistant at Deacon's Lodge Golf Course for the last 26 years. He is an 11-time club champion at the Cuyuna Country Club in Deerwood.

1970 Billy Fawcett champion, Rich Aulie

Aulie would go on to coach the boys' golf team at Crosby-Ironton High School for 37 years. His 1996 team won the Class A state championship. Rich is a member of the Minnesota Golf Coaches Hall of Fame and now lives on the third hole at Breezy Point's Traditional Golf Course.

Breezy Point golf course manager Doug Nelson gave former champion Don Heidt another putting lesson in the 1971 finals. Nelson made five 3s in the first six holes to pile up an insurmountable lead, closing out Heidt on the 11th hole 8 & 7. He was four under par when the match ended. A member of the 1966 North Branch High School state championship golf team, Doug worked in the pro shop at Breezy Point and served as the golf professional here in the early 1970s.

HOLE	1	2	3	4	5	6	7	8	9	Out	10	11	12	13	14	15	16	17	18	In	Total	Hdcp.	Ne
YARDS	317	162	263	288	398	163	362	352	370	2681	362	193	313	180	306	386	327	366	365	2782	5463		
MEN'S PAR	4	3	4	4	4	3	4	4	4	34	4	3	4	4	4	4	4	4	4	34	68		
WOMEN'S PAR	4	3	4	4	4	3	4	5	5	36	4	3	4	3	4	5	4	4	5	36	72		
Heidt	4	3	4	6	6	4	4	4	4	39	5	4											
Nelson	3	3	3	4	3	3	4	3	4	30	4	3											
MEN'S HDCP.	12	14	18	17	1	10	3	7	5		9	6	13	15	16	2	11	8	4				

Original Scorecard from the 1971 final match, provided by Doug Nelson. Seven threes in 11 holes! No wonder he became a professional golfer.

1975 champion R.J. Smiley

An NAIA All-American golfer at Fort Hays College in the 1960s, R.J. Smiley defeated Mac Alexander to win the 1975 Billy Fawcett tournament. R.J. went on to win the Minnesota Senior Public Links in 1997 and the Minnesota Senior Amateur title in 1998.

Smiley was a medalist at the Pine to Palm in 1978 and reached the semifinals there twice in the 1970s. Owner of the Mille Lacs Golf Course from 1983 to 2004, he ran his own invitational tournament there that attracted many of the top golfers in the state. R.J. also helped develop other golf courses in the state, including the Links at North Fork, Pheasant Acres, and Blueberry Pines. A freelance writer since 2008, Smiley also serves as the director of Ace Golf Technologies.

After graduating from Kent State University in 1974, Dan Strimple and his wife, Jan, set off on a two-year honeymoon trip across the United States. They spent the winter of 1976 in Phoenix, Arizona, where Dan caddied at the Phoenix Country Club and hung out with Breezy Point professional Doug Nelson. Nelson offered Strimple a job as his assistant, so in the summer of 1976, Dan was behind the counter in the golf shop while Jan worked as a hostess at the Marina restaurant.

One of the first people Strimple met after starting work was Bob Ylinen, who asked him if he wanted to play golf with some money on the line. Not knowing what to expect, the former division-one college golfer offered to play Ylinen straight up using only a 7-iron and a putter while Bob played with his full set of golf clubs. In a scene straight out of *Caddyshack*, Dan remembered they played for $5 a hole, with Strimple taking $45 from Ylinen that day.

In August of 1976, Doug Nelson left Breezy Point to take a job in Rapid City, South Dakota. Dan took over as the pro shop manager and would play in and help run the Billy Fawcett Match Play Tournament over Labor Day weekend. The tournament had a record 92 entrants.

Strimple shot a 72 in the qualifying round before going through the match-play portion of the tournament like a buzzsaw. Dan defeated Jerry Whalen 4 & 2 in the quarterfinals and Mark Alexander 8 & 6 in the semifinals. Alexander would win the Fawcett tournament in 1981, while Whalen would capture the title in both 1982 and 1985.

Dan faced defending champion R.J. Smiley in the finals. He built up an insurmountable lead after firing a 30 on the front nine. Forced to play catch up, Smiley took out his driver and drove his ball onto the green on the par 4 12th hole. His two-putt birdie won the hole, but it was too little too late. Strimple kept the pedal down and closed out the match 5 & 4 on the 14th green after a remarkable display of putting.

At a cocktail party after the tournament, Dan remembers R.J. Smiley telling him, "I don't like the way you putt!" He also remembers Erv Pental giving him $100, 10% of Erv's winnings from the tournament's pari-mutuel, and Mac McChesney taking Dan and his wife to Bar Harbor for a celebratory dinner afterward. Mac probably also celebrated his consolation championship in the sixth flight that year.

Sports columnist Bob Utecht, the voice of Minnesota North Stars hockey, wrote this in his *Bloomington Sun* column after the tournament was over:

Among the nation's youthful amateur golfers that you're going to be hearing about will be one Dan Strimple, assistant at Breezy Point the past summer. Dan won the annual Billy Fawcett Open with impressive golf in beating R.J. Smiley, the defending champ in match play. Most impressive was Dan's shooting 30 on the front nine. The past week he proved himself again by taking second in the North Dakota Open. You'll be hearing more from this lean, lanky young man with the big swing and the soft touch around the greens.

The Strimples settled in Dallas, Texas, in 1981 but continued to travel, Jan as a high-end model and Dan as a professional golfer. He would make it to the PGA Tour qualifying final stage in 1983, played on the minor league Ben Hogan tour for a time, and made some PGA Tour starts through Monday qualifying. In 1986, after working at several country clubs, Strimple found a home at the Irving Golf Range in Dallas as a teaching professional and founder of the Fundamental Golf School. Dan was named the North Texas

PGA Teacher of the Year in 1994 and 1996. In 1998, he was ranked one of the top five teaching professionals in the Dallas area together with Tiger Woods' future coach Hank Haney and Scottie Scheffler's instructor Randy Smith.

Dan Strimple displays the putting form that carried him to the title in 1976.

After losing in the semifinals in 1978, John Hoffman was a man on a mission in 1979 and had his golf game dialed in. John remembers winning a sizable bet with Terry Sopko in a practice round before the tournament that paid for his entry fee. He went on to beat Sopko in the semifinals, 2 &1. It was his closest match of the tournament. Hoffman got ahead early in the finals against defending champion Chuck Meyer and did not allow the match to come back across the road as he closed out Meyer on the 15th green, 4 & 3. John also won the first Breezy Point Invitational, a 54-hole stroke play tournament started in 1980. Hoffman has qualified for five different USGA events including the Junior, Amateur, Mid-

Am, and Senior Am. John remembers playing with future PGA stars Scott Simpson and Scott Hoch in the 1973 USGA Junior. He also has played in the British Mid Am and the Australian Senior Amateur, and today remains a very competitive senior golfer in Southern California.

John Hoffman with the Billy Fawcett trophy he won 40 years ago

In 1980, 16-year-old Joe Towle qualified for the championship flight for the first time and rode his short game to the finals, where he took on local favorite and defending champion, John Hoffman. Towle remembers warming up on the old par-3 course down by the lake before the match.

On the third hole, Hoffman drove the green on the 263-yard par-4. Joe's caddie, 1978 champ Chuck Meyer, advised him to lay up with an iron, leaving him a second shot of 60 yards.

Drawing on the short wedges he had hit warming up on the par-3 course, Towle holed out his second shot for an eagle to win the hole. He carried that 1-up lead to the 18th hole where both golfers made par, giving Joe a 1-up victory. He would be only the sixth teenager to win the Breezy Point championship.

Towle also went on to win the Breezy Point Invitational, a 54-hole stroke-play event, five years in a row from 1981 to 1985. Jean Lindell defeated Jean Alexander to win her fourth ladies' title in a row in 1980, breaking the ladies' record of three in a row set by Mrs. Ralph Little and Patty Berg a half-century earlier.

1977-1980 Ladies' champion Jean Lindell. Four in a row, and a new record for women!

Ms. Lindell, who was crowned Miss Brainerd in 1949, was a member at Southview C.C. in St. Paul and competed frequently in the Minnesota Senior Women's Amateur in the 1980s. She would eventually win the Breezy Point tournament six times to tie Mrs. Ralph Little for most championships won.

Jean Lindell, Jean Alexander, and Pat Bartholomew would dominate the women's division in the 1970s and 80s, collectively winning the ladies' championship 11 times and usually competing against one another in the finals.

The Boxer...

NEW BOXING PROMOTER IN TWIN CITIES

NOTED SPORTSMAN, PUBLISHER, PURCHASES FRAN-CHISES

FORMS ORGANIZATION, TWIN CITIES ATHLETIC ASSO-CIATION

NEW FIGHT PROMOTER IN THE TWIN CITIES

CAPT. WILLIAM FAWCETT is the new boxing promoter in the Twin Cities. The above picture was taken just before he left for France.

Captain Billy Fawcett was a boxing fan who attended many of the major heavyweight fights held in the 1920s. A friend of the great Jack Dempsey, he hosted the champion heavyweight at Breezy Point in December of 1931. Dempsey spent two days training here after an exhibition match at Fargo, doing six miles of road work each day before traveling to Duluth for another exhibition match. Captain Fawcett hosted a dinner for Dempsey attended by a few Brainerd businessmen before sending him on his way. Captain Billy had a short career as a boxing promoter when he purchased both the Minneapolis and St. Paul boxing clubs in 1925 and created the Twin Cities Athletic Association. Fawcett hired boxing promoter Jack Reddy to help him manage the business, but things fell apart in April of 1926 when Reddy scheduled an unauthorized fight without Fawcett's knowledge. Reddy was suspended by the Minnesota Boxing Commission, and Fawcett decided to sell his interest in the club.

FROM RING TO TEE FOR GIBBONS

Boxer Jack Gibbons with golf pros Elmer Carlson and Norman Clark at the 1938 St. Paul Open

Captain Fawcett had originally wanted former boxer Mike Gibbons as the club manager, but Gibbons decided he didn't want to take that on. Gibbons' son, Jack, was the fourth-ranked middleweight in the world in 1935. Jack Gibbons was a natural athlete who also knew how to play golf. After defeating Frank Battaglia in a middleweight bout in 1935, Jack vacationed at Breezy Point and played golf with Billy Fawcett at his Breezy Point course. When Jack got married in 1938, he quit boxing. He went on to become an accomplished boxing referee and was appointed to the Minnesota Boxing Commission in 1965. He took his golf seriously and would hit practice balls for hours at a time. The picture on the opposite page shows Gibbons competing in the PGA Tour's St. Paul Open in 1938.

Qualifying for the Minnesota Amateur in 1950, Gibbons went on to win his first two matches before being defeated in the semifinals. Jack had a summer home on Gull Lake and enjoyed playing in the Camp Confidence tournament during its early years. He was the low celebrity golfer in 1975, with a 78. He also recorded a third-place finish in the 1960 Brainerd Shortstop Tournament. After a short bout with Alzheimer's, Gibbons passed away in Brainerd in 1999.

Minnesota heavyweight Jim Beattie chose Breezy Point as the training site for his bout with Buster Mathis in 1968. Although he wasn't much of a golfer, Beattie set up his training ring next to the first tee at the Breezy Point golf course. His daily routine involved four or five miles of road work before a 10 a.m. breakfast, sparring in the ring at the golf course at 1:30, and a second and final meal of the day at 4 p.m.

The training at Breezy Point went well. The fight with Mathis was not so good. Beattie lost the fight in a seventh-round TKO.

Crosby's Scott LeDoux was another boxer who was a good all-around athlete. LeDoux played college football at UMD before trying his hand at boxing. He was one of Jim Beattie's sparring partners at Breezy Point in 1968. During a successful boxing career that included two heavyweight championship fights, LeDoux came to Breezy Point in 1977 to take part in their celebrity golf tournament. Scott ran four miles and staged workouts both days with Minneapolis boxer Louie Hokenson, Minnesota Vikings Dave Osborn, Mick Tingelhoff, Bob Lurtsema, and "some guy out of the crowd" as opponents. He also shot a respectable 71 in the golf tournament.

Jim Beattie is reduced to working out with a small punching bag when a Breezy Point pine tree couldn't hold his heavy bag after taking a couple strong punches from Beattie.

A Breezy Point property owner, LeDoux returned in 1979 to train for his heavyweight title fight with Mike Weaver. Scott lost a unanimous decision to Weaver but continued to box until retiring in 1985. He died in 2011 after a three-year battle with Lou Gehrig's disease (ALS).

Jack Slavin

Jack Slavin was a fine amateur boxer who twice won the Minneapolis Golden Gloves title at 135 pounds and had four professional bouts in the 1940s. Jack's brother, Jerry, is a member of the Minnesota Boxing Hall of Fame. After retiring as the owner of a vending machine business, Slavin moved to Breezy Point in 1985. Jack made eight holes-in-one in a five-year period from 1985 to 1990 and holds the record for most holes-in-one by a golfer connected to the Breezy Point area.

Breezy Point was the site of the world's fastest hole of golf in July of 2018 when another Crosby boxer, Rick Aulie, played the 503-yard fourth hole at Whitebirch Golf Course in one minute and 39.2 seconds to claim the Guinness World Record. Aulie was a

U.S.A. boxing state champion who made it to the Upper Midwest Golden Gloves Finals at 141 pounds in both 2002 and 2003. Retired from boxing, Rick now trains for marathons, doing his roadwork on some of the same trails Jack Dempsey ran during his 1931 visit to Breezy Point. Aulie plays golf at the Breezy Point golf courses and has a personal best score of 66 from the tips at Whitebirch.

Many professional athletes have turned to golf when their playing careers are finished. Minnesota Vikings safety Paul Krause was an excellent golfer who won the Breezy Point Celebrity Tournament twice, shooting a 71 in 1976 and a 67 in 1977. Krause also competed in the Breezy Point Invitational in the 1980s.

Paul Krause, young Chris Perry, and dad Jim Perry in 1977

It should be noted that Krause was tied for first-place honors both years by young Chris Perry, son of Minnesota Twins pitcher Jim Perry. Chris went on to win the Minnesota High School golf championship three years in a row from 1978 to 1980 while playing for Edina High School. Perry played college golf at Ohio State University and then competed on the PGA Tour, where he won the 1998 BC Open. He won the Minnesota State Amateur in 1982 and

1983, and the State Open in 1984 before turning pro.

I remember playing in the Minnesota Amateur at Detroit Lakes in 1983. In my first tournament round since high school, I opened with a 73, the same score as defending champion Chris Perry. I felt pretty good about my score. Chris, however, told the newspaper it was his "worst round of the year." On the second day, there was a rain delay after nine holes. Checking the scoreboard, I noticed Perry and I had both shot 35 and were still tied after 27 holes. Perry went on to shoot 67-68 to win the tournament while I finished 74-76 and tied for 20th. We both had a good tournament, and I got a firsthand look at the difference between my golf game and that of an aspiring tour professional.

Minnesota Twins outfielder Bob Allison had a home on the 5th hole at the Traditional course and competed in the Billy Fawcett tournament on occasion. When the onset of ataxia began to limit his mobility, Rob Birkeland and Chuck Meyer would put Allison in their golf cart when they went out to play the Traditional course. Bob would provide a running commentary and trash talk while Birkeland, Meyer, and Allison's former teammate Rich Reese competed against one another. Breezy Point held the Bob Allison Celebrity Tournament from 1993 to 1996 to benefit ataxia research. Sadly, Bob passed away in 1995 from complications brought on by the disease.

Minnesota Twins first baseman Rich Reese, a good friend of Allison, was a member at Deacon's Lodge for many years and won the Charlie's Scramble tournament on occasion, including a 9-under-par 27 with partners Steve Stoxen and Rob Birkeland in 1994. Former Twins pitcher and World Series star Jack Morris played at Deacon's in 1999. Morris had arms that looked as big as around as my legs! His drive on hole one from the blue tees was a bullet that ended up near the tall pine tree just left of the first green, 375 yards away. Strike three, you're out! Former Washington Redskins kicker Chip Lohmiller plays quite frequently at Deacon's and has a personal best score of 67 there.

Bob Allison watching play in the 1993 tournament.

Defenseman Shawn Chambers won the Stanley Cup while playing for the New Jersey Devils in 1995 and again with the Dallas Stars in 1999. Shawn is one of the better golfers among the former pro athletes who play at Breezy Point. Chambers has competed in the Minnesota State Open and won a first-round match in the MGA Players Championship when it was held at Deacon's in 2011. Shawn also more than holds his own against the local pros and top area amateurs who play a regular Tuesday money game at different area courses during the summer. He plays from the back tees and can shoot close to par whenever he tees it up.

In 2013, a group of 28 basketball coaches from Texas came to play at Deacon's Lodge. While I was starting their group on the first tee, one of the coaches began telling me about the courses they had already played on their trip: Hazeltine, Interlachen, the

Classic, and the Preserve. In the coming days, they would play at Giant's Ridge and at Northland Country Club in Duluth. When I asked him who had set up their trip, he told me, "Coach's daughter set it up, but Coach had to make some of the calls." Since they were all basketball coaches, I asked him who he was talking about, and he pointed back to the tall gentleman in the back sitting in a golf cart: Bobby Knight.

The author with coach Bob Knight at Deacon's Lodge in 2013.

A short time later, after an autograph and the requisite picture, I found Coach Knight's group on the short par-3 sixth hole at Deacon's. From the top of the hill, I observed Knight top his ball into the waste bunker in front of the tee. That was followed by the signature "chair toss" as his wedge followed the ball into the bunker. With discretion being the better part of valor, I turned my cart around and headed toward another hole.

Chapter 8: The Decade of Greed

"Greed is good!" –Gordon Gekko, *Wall Street* (1987)

The 1980s were a time when everything was bigger and brighter. Hair was high and fashion was loud. Former movie star Ronald Reagan was elected president after promising to reduce government spending, taxes, and regulation. He wanted to get government out of the way and allow the forces of supply and demand to rule the market. As the American economy began to pull out of the 1970s recession, Breezy Point was ready to go.

Robert "Bob" Spizzo came to Breezy Point in 1977 at the bequest of his friend Jerry Lenz to give the Whitebirch development a kick start. Spizzo wanted to introduce a time-share concept that allowed people to own weekly shares of time at various resort properties. Time-sharing was a completely new concept in Minnesota, and the Hopkins House group decided to pass on the idea. Spizzo and Lenz offered to buy out Hopkins House's share of Whitebirch in 1981, and Hopkins House countered with an offer to sell both their Whitebirch interest and the resort. The deal was consummated, and a new era was ready to begin at Breezy Point. Although Bob Spizzo didn't have the deep pockets of Breezy's founder Billy Fawcett, he did share Fawcett's vision for what the resort could be and was ready to get to work. Among the items at the top of his list was a new golf course.

The Championship Course: Whitebirch

Hole sixteen at Whitebirch Golf Course

Whitebirch, Inc. was established in 1974 with a plan to develop 3,000 acres of woodland next to Breezy Point Resort. The plan included single-family subdivisions, a campground, and Minnesota's first timeshares. An 18-hole championship golf course was also a part of that plan.

The golf course was designed by Dexter Hubbard, a landscape architect from Fredericksburg, Virginia, with the course laid out and staked by Landecker and Associates of Pequot Lakes, led by Myron (Mike) Landecker. The clearing and grubbing were done by Brad Lenz, son of Jerry Lenz, a partner in the Whitebirch development. The shaper, using an older machine, worked slowly and sometimes would only work when he felt like it. Bob Spizzo found he could get a little more work out of him if he sent a plate of cookies over, so that became part of the daily routine.

Golf course construction started in the late 1970s. The picture below shows Mike Landecker checking on the construction progress near the green complex on Hole Number 8. The photo was taken by architect Dexter Hubbard.

MYRON (MIKE) LANDECKER
*Checking construction on hole eight at the
Championship GC in 1979.*

The front nine opened for play in 1982 and was called the Championship course to differentiate it from the shorter Traditional golf course. The photo below shows the golf carts lined up alongside the first tee as golfers teed off on opening day. With the opening of the new nine, Breezy Point now had 27 regular holes plus a nine-hole par-3 course down by the lake.

Father Edward Ramacher hits the opening tee shot at the Championship course in August of 1982 while Delores Calder, Jim Harmon, and Amy Cronin look on.

While Breezy was building their new course, there was more going on behind the scenes. In 1983, a group of investors, which included some Oklahoma oilmen, purchased 500 acres of land just north of the Breezy Point Resort. Some of the investors were members of Pete Dye's famous Oak Tree National Golf Club in Edmund, Oklahoma, and wanted to build their own version of that course here in Minnesota. Their Pine Tree Golf and Country Club would be a gated community with its own private golf course. While the Pine Tree investors struggled to get public approval and the necessary permits to begin building, Breezy Point continued work on the second nine holes at their Championship course.

The back nine was completed in 1989, giving Breezy Point a championship par-72 golf course that played at 6,680 yards. Additional tees were added later, giving players four sets of tees to choose from to find a course length that fit their game. The course now plays anywhere from 4,750 yards at the forward tees to 6,730 yards from the back tees.

A new clubhouse was added in 1996. Bringing back memories of Susan and Keith at the piano bar in the historic log building by the lake, the restaurant and bar in the new clubhouse was called Antlers. In another blast from the past, 1983 Billy Fawcett Tournament champion Tony Palaia supervised the construction work. Along with the new clubhouse came a new name for the golf course. Drawing from the development surrounding the course, the Championship course now became known as Whitebirch Golf Course.

Whitebirch clubhouse and the Antlers bar and restaurant

The Texas Scramble

A scramble is a team competition in golf where each player on the team hits a drive, the best drive is selected, and everyone plays the next shot from that point. The team continues that process until their ball is holed out. It was originally called "Captain's Choice," as the best player in each group would make the decision on which shot would be taken for the next stroke. It also became known as a "Texas Scramble" when it took off in that state during the Depression. The Texas Scramble became the game of choice for gamblers in Las Vegas during the 1950s.

I was introduced to the Texas Scramble in the 1980s by a man at my golf club named Gene Schadow. "Shady" was an inveterate gambler who liked to have a little money riding on whatever competition he was involved in. He was overseeing our club's games committee when he introduced us to the Texas Scramble. Each four-player team was required to have one low-handicap golfer, two medium-handicap golfers, and one high-handicap golfer. Every player on the team had to use their tee shot a minimum number of times to keep everyone involved and even out the competition somewhat. The Scramble became extremely popular at our club. Pretty soon, after 18 holes on men's day, a few golfers would gather on the first tee, choose up sides, and head out for a fun four-hole scramble with a few dollars on the line. It's a tradition that continues to this day, almost 40 years later!

At about the same time, Dick Garn founded the Oldsmobile Scramble. It eventually grew to become the world's largest national golf tournament. Over 1.5 million golfers have participated in an Oldsmobile Scramble local tournament since its inception in 1984. More than 2,100 local tournaments were held each year in 48 states.

Local qualifiers were joined by the host pro at each site when they competed in the section tournament. Section winners qualified for the national tournament at Walt Disney World and were joined there by a player from the PGA Tour if their team made the final cut.

Each team was made up of a low-handicap or A player, two slightly higher handicapped B and C players, and a high-handicap D player. Every player on the team was required to use their drive at least twice in the 18-hole round.

Mark Neva of Deacon's Lodge took two teams to the national tournament in Orlando while he was working at the Pines at Grandview. In 1993, the Pines team of Kevin Cashman, Tom Kientzle, Steve Stoxen, and Fred and Carolyn Boos made it to the national tournament, becoming the first team from Minnesota to qualify for the finals.

Playing with PGA Tour professional Jim Hallet, they finished fourth overall in the net division but shot the low score on the final day with a 19-under-par 53, good for a net score of 22-under-par 50! First place in the final round was worth $15,000 to the low pro, Hallet, and $2,000 to the Pines course pro, Cashman. Out of all the team's great shots that day, probably the best was Carolyn Boos' 85-foot putt for an eagle on one of the par-5s.

It was during the decade of greed that the Texas Scramble became the game of choice at Breezy Point. Joe Doty's Edgewater Inn tournament had its beginning in September of 1982. The golf was oftentimes secondary to the dinner and Calcutta held the night before the tournament. Each four-man team was made up of an A, B, C, and D player determined by their handicap number. The names were randomly drawn out of a box by Father Ramacher. Once the names were drawn, the Calcutta would begin, and teams were auctioned off.

It was always good to know who the players were on your team before the bidding started. A prominent businessman once asked Dave Gravdahl who his A-player, or top player, was. As Dave pointed him out, the highly intoxicated golfer passed out and fell to the floor.

The Calcutta usually totaled between $125,000 and $175,000. With no bank open on the weekend, the local sheriff would hold the money overnight for safekeeping. Played on the Traditional Course, the Edgewater tournament had its own unique twist—only the A-player could putt on hole 4, only the B-player on hole 7, and only the C-player on hole 15.

With the holes cut on the severe slopes of these greens, scores could drastically change as golfers' hands began to shake over short putts that could be worth tens of thousands of dollars. The Edgewater had its springtime counterpart in the Run-Amuck tournament, put on in May by a group of summer residents from Oklahoma.

Part party and part golf tournament, the Run-Amuck featured live music at the Championship golf course and a helicopter flying over the course filming the play, no doubt keeping an eye out for any cheaters!

Like the Edgewater tournament, the Run-Amuck also had a large Calcutta payoff for the winners. These tournaments would come and go, but one scramble event has survived for over 40 years now at Breezy Point thanks to a man from Iowa named Charlie.

Charlie Paige, a native of Dike, Iowa, was a natural-born organizer. A real people person, Charlie helped manage Charlie's Saloon and Rib Joint during his summers in Breezy Point. If he wasn't at the restaurant, you could find Charlie and his wife, Rosella, at the golf course.

Tuesday night business at the restaurant was slow and needed a shot in the arm, so the Tuesday afternoon scramble with dinner was born. Charlie devised a simple format for the competition. Teams consisted of three players with no handicap restrictions. Equal numbered flights were set up for all teams after all the scores were turned in. Everyone had a chance to win with the luck of the draw, regardless of what their score was. The prize money was spread around, which kept players returning time after time. Don't have a partner for the scramble? No problem. Charlie would line you up with a team and had a great knack for putting like-minded people together.

I have enjoyed competing in Charlie's Scramble for over 30 years now with my partners Bill Stein and Mike Patterson of Aitkin. The golf is fun, the friendships are genuine, and the steak dinner after the round prepared by chef Dave Gravdahl provides the end to a perfect day of golf. In the late 1990s, the team of Stein, Patterson, and Aulie shot a 9-under-par 27 on the back nine in August and a 9-under 27 on the front nine in September to claim the first-place money two months in a row.

182

That, however, is not the record for a Charlie's Scramble. Between 1984 and 1986, the team of Greg Johnson and Steve Stoxen of Brainerd and Tim Dullum of Nisswa took first place overall for six consecutive months! Included in one of those wins was a 10-under-par 26 to set the record score for Charlie's Scramble. Kai Peterson and Twin Cities friends Schroeder and Herbert also shot a 10-under score in 1998. Breezy Point's director of golf, Mark Johnson, recalls teaming up with Greg Johnson and Scott Kleberg to also shoot 10-under, and Jesse Nelson recalls the Deacon's Lodge team (Nelson, Josh Dale, and Brian Melberg) also getting to 10-under once.

1997 Charlie's Scramble picture. Checking the golfers in are Pat Brennan, Rosella Paige, and PGA pro Ken Lubke, with organizer Charlie Paige standing behind them.

June of 2000 was the last Charlie's Scramble with Charlie in attendance. He and Rosella sold their home and went on to spend their summers in Iowa and their winters in Arizona. Rosella passed away in 2012, and Charlie in February of 2022 at the age of 95! Breezy Point's Mark Johnson took over the reins and has kept the tournament going for over 20 years now. It is still known as Charlie's Scramble, always the first Tuesday of the month during the summer.

Caddyshack Too: Golf at Breezy Point in the 1980s

Charlie Paige wasn't the only character at Breezy Point in the 1980s. Everyone I've talked with has referred to golf in the 1980s at Breezy Point as resembling a classic golf movie. *Caddyshack* was first released in 1980 to mixed reviews.

Over the years, it has developed a cult following that includes golfer Tiger Woods. In 2014, American Express shot a commercial parody based on *Caddyshack* with Woods playing the part of greenskeeper Carl Spackler.

The film was described by ESPN as "Perhaps the funniest sports movie of all time. It still ranks as the most quotable sports film."

Like the Marx Brothers spoof of college football, *Horsefeathers*, much of the movie was unscripted and relied on improvisation. The actors had the freedom to wander off in all directions in search of comic inspiration.

Like many successful films, there was a sequel, *Caddyshack II*, released in 1988. It did poorly at the box office and is considered one of the worst sequels of all time!

The real sequel should have been made at Breezy Point, where *Caddyshack* was alive and well, living out the golfer's dream in the 1980s.

Bob Kroiss

"Let's go. While we're young!"

Rodney Dangerfield's character, Al Czervik, was inhabited by Minneapolis businessman and Pelican Lake resident Bob Kroiss.

An 18-handicap golfer, Bob was a member at Midland Hills in the cities and at Scottsdale CC in Arizona during the winter. He shot his age for six consecutive years beginning at age 74 and recorded six holes in one, including one on hole 13 at Breezy's Traditional course. Kroiss was a member of the West Bank Sportsman's Club, a group that played regularly on Saturday mornings at the Traditional course. Bob would show up with flags and streamers hanging from his cart and a horn he would beep whenever the spirit moved him. Kroiss was the man who stirred the drink and made things happen as he directed all the fun and games for the group. Rob Birkeland remembers Kroiss had a unique golf swing that produced one of two shots he called the "Michigan Knockdown" and the "Feather Floater." Don Peddie said he could chip and putt with the best of them and knew how to keep his ball in play. Plus, he knew every blade of grass on the Breezy Point course, where at one time he either owned or had an interest in several parcels of land.

Chuck Meyer

"Two wrongs don't make a right, but three rights make a left."

The part of Chevy Chase's character, Ty Webb, belonged to Chuck Meyer, a clone of professional golfer Peter Jacobson. Chuck lived comfortably in both the happy-go-lucky and the competitive golf world and could travel back and forth between the two whenever the situation called for it. Meyer was the Billy Fawcett champion in 1978 and 1986 and competed in the Breezy Point Invitational for many years, finishing second in 1980 and 1990. Chuck was a tough match-play competitor with a game well suited for the tight fairways at Breezy Point's Traditional course. Meyer's extremely short swing was repeatable and produced very straight shots. Childhood friend Jeff Arundel recalled that Chuck usually hit the ground first and drop-kicked his driver about 220 yards right down the middle of the fairway. He was also a very good putter who made five-foot putts like clockwork, even on the severely sloping greens on the Traditional course.

Playing together in the summer at Breezy, Arundel and Meyer played mythical Billy Fawcett matches to prepare for the annual Labor Day tournament. Joe Towle remembered Meyer was particularly adept at reading the tell-tale signs that showed when an opponent might be ready to fold. When Bob Terri started to hook the ball, for example, Chuck always said it was time to double the bet. Meyer was an excellent guitar player as well as a master storyteller well-liked by everyone. In the age of polyester fashions, Chuck Meyer was the Prince of Breezy Point.

1986 Billy Fawcett Tournament participants. Champion Chuck Meyer, in the front row, holding the most important trophy: his young child!

Mac McChesney

"Gambling is not allowed at Breezy Point, sir, and I never slice!"

Ted Knight's character, Judge Smails, would have been found in Mac McChesney. Mac helped to start and/or run many of the tournaments at Breezy Point in the 70s and 80s, including the Billy Fawcett tournament, the Sunday Scrambles, Charlie's Scramble, the Men's Traveling League, and the Breezy Point Invitational (later known as the Orv Invitational). A member at St. Cloud CC, McChesney was well versed in the rules of golf and could be counted on to make a ruling in the absence of a golf professional during his time at Breezy. He was an organizer and a taskmaster.

In the early 1970s, as residential developments were starting up around Breezy Point, golf course starter Frank Cronin and his wife, Amy, along with Ken Gilbert and Mac McChesney, came up with an idea for a social gathering on Sunday afternoons. The Couples Scramble with four players on a team was born, and it continues to this day. Nine holes of golf followed by 19th-hole refreshments at a nearby home comprised the format and over the years proved to be very successful. In June of 1976, the *Lake Country Echo* noted the couples' scramble was followed by a steak fry with music provided by longtime Breezy entertainers Susan and Keith. The last-place team was awarded the "Burnt Club Award" with the inscription *You Gotta Get Hotter!*

Golf course manager Orv Hagen adopted the idea in the 1980s and promoted it with leadership from Fred Rogers of Camp Lincoln and Breezy Point's McChesney. It became a spontaneous Sunday affair starting at 3:00 p.m., featuring low-key, semi-serious golf with friends followed by 19th-hole festivities at a nearby home.

The Rogers (Fred and Marlys) maintained a Breezy connection when Brownie Cote sold the resort in the early 1960s. Cote put a golf privilege clause in the sales agreement giving Grand View Lodge family members playing rights. Along with the Rogers, Cote's wife, Julia, a frequent competitor at Breezy Point over the years, played quite often with the Sunday group. She would partner with her husband, daughter Mary, or Mary's husband, Fred Boos.

The Couple's Scramble has continued to survive quite nicely through the years. Newcomers were always welcome, and you didn't have to live near the course. Golf was secondary to having a good time, but there were always some good players competing. Terry Sopko and wife, Ann, combined with Earle and Bev Wooley to shoot a record round of 26 8-under-par in the 1980s!

Reporting on the Sunday Scramble in 1997, Don Peddie said, "If you want to make a prediction about golf at Breezy Point, the first thing to say is that there always will be a Sunday Couples Scramble." This photo, taken in 2021, will attest to the veracity of that statement.

A typical Sunday scene with the carts lined up behind the ninth green after the round. Time for socializing.

Joe Towle
"Be the ball, Danny. Be the ball."

Joe Towle at the old Par-3 course by Pelican Lake

Caddie Danny Noonan was well represented by Joe Towle at Breezy Point. Joe worked several jobs during his time at Breezy including cart boy, golf shop assistant, bartender, and bag man! His jobs left him privy to most of the shenanigans at the golf course during the early 80s.

Towle said most days were a microcosm of the *Caddyshack* movie. Joe could also play a bit, winning the Billy Fawcett tournament as a 16-year-old in 1980. He was among a very good group of young golfers who played at Breezy Point in the early 1980s including John and Peter Hoffman, Peter and Rob Birkeland, and Greg Johnson.

Many of them got their start at Breezy playing the old par-3 course down by the lake before later taking on the sharks at the regular course. Peter Hoffman shot 66, 64, 64, and 61 in a week one summer and said he had trouble getting a game with anyone for the rest of the year. It also probably didn't help that Hoffman and his friend Rob Birkland had a credit card machine mounted on their golf cart!

John Hoffman has competed in five USGA national tournaments while brother Peter and Greg Johnson went on to play professionally. Together with Towle, those four captured the Breezy Invitational title 11 times!

Ever since Captain Billy started the Ten Thousand Lakes golf tournament, it has been a favorite tournament for younger players. Fawcett wanted it that way and did everything possible to get younger golfers into the field. It was at Breezy Point where a 17-year-old Les Bolstad first started to shine. Later, Fawcett would finance him in his first venture into professional tournament golf. Besides Bolstad, other teenagers who have won the Ten Thousand Lakes Tournament include Art Tverra in 1926, Patty Berg in 1933-1935, Berg's brother Herman in 1939, Rich Aulie in 1970, and Joe Towle in 1980.

Henry Ordemann

"So, I got that going for me, which is nice."

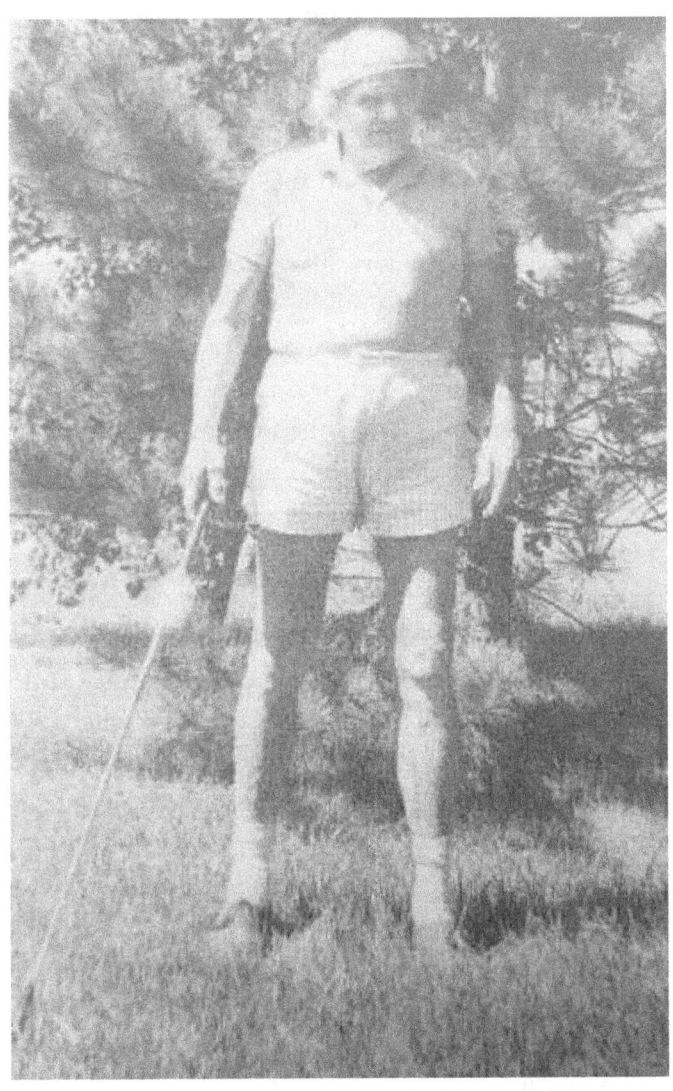

No one represented the *Caddyshack* era at Breezy Point better than Henry Ordemann, Breezy's answer to greenskeeper Carl Spackler. On June 23, 1980, Henry played 102 holes in one day on the Traditional golf course. In June of 1981, Henry went out to try and break his record from the previous year. In the spirit of *Caddyshack*, there was a $1,000 bet on whether Ordemann could beat his own record. The 64-year-old resident of Richfield started at 4:45 a.m. on the longest day of the year and finished 130 holes later at 7:30 p.m. Walking the entire distance, a little over 21 miles, his average score for the day was in the low 80s. Afterward, Ordemann stated that he planned to play golf until he had to ride around in a cart like these kids in their 20s, pointing to caddie Joe Towle riding along in a golf cart. Young Towle was entrusted to hold the money from the bet and paid off Henry when the marathon was finished.

Inspired by his accomplishment, Ordemann continued the golf marathon for several more years at different area golf courses. Henry played 135 holes at the Brainerd CC in 1982, scoring two birdies on one hole. On hole 11, his ball collided with a swallow before continuing to the green. The bird got up and flew away, and Ordemann went on to sink his putt for another birdie! In 1986, he played 225 holes at Mille Lacs Golf Resort for a personal record. His final marathon was in 1987 at the age of 70.

Henry and Breezy Point bartender Brett Dale played 200 holes in a two-man scramble at Birch Bay Golf Course. Beginning at 5:25 a.m., they finished up at 10:00 p.m., using flashlights to navigate the last 11 holes.

Henry was once asked why he took on the grueling golf marathon. In true Carl Spackler fashion, Ordemann said, "I love the game, but it's also like bullfighting—that's goofier yet. Or driving a car over 200 miles an hour. I guess it's a personal mountain for me." Hopefully, Henry found the Dalai Lama at the top of his mountain and received total consciousness. "Gunga lagunga. Gunga gunga-lagunga!"

Orv Hagen

"There's been a lot of complaints already. If you want to get fired. If you want to be replaced by golf carts, keep it up."

Orv Hagen (no relation to Sir Walter) started working at Breezy Point in 1977 as a chef at the supper club. He had previously worked in kitchens all over the U.S. and also spent some time as a carnival worker riding motorcycles in a barrel. He never did anything in moderation.

Orv was on duty the night in June when lightning struck the resort and the supper club burned down. He went on to become the golf course manager at Breezy Point in the late 1970s and 1980s. Along with Mac McChesney, Orv was responsible for organizing and running many of the tournaments held at Breezy Point. He helped the resort transition from an 18-hole to a 36-hole facility with the opening of the Championship Golf Course in 1982. Orv also started the Breezy Point Invitational tournament in 1980 for area professionals and top amateurs. It became known as "Orv's Invitational" and consisted of a select field of 12 golfers who played 54 holes of golf over two days. Most of the rounds were played on the Traditional Golf Course, but beginning in 1983, at least nine holes were played on the new Championship Course. When the back nine of the Championship course opened in 1989, 27 holes were played at both courses. On Saturday, golf might be nine holes at Traditional followed by 18 holes at Championship.

Sunday began with nine holes at Championship and ended with a full 18 at Traditional. It was interesting that through the years, the par-68 Traditional course would only play about one stroke lower than the par-72 Championship course, even though there was a four-stroke difference in their par.

Breezy Point's Joe Towle won the invitational five years in a row from 1981 to 1985. Pro Scott Sorum won the tournament in 1997 to tie Towle with five titles. Pros with Breezy Point ties did well over the years. Breezy assistant pro and mini-tour player Greg "Kegger" Johnson won three times, including a tournament record score of 212 in 1996.

Rush Creek pro Peter Hoffman grew up playing golf at Breezy Point and would win the tournament twice along with four second-place finishes. Pete recalled that his student and friend Tim "Lumpy" Herron was scheduled to play here in 1992 but lost his chance at an invite after winning the state amateur tournament that summer. Orv Hagen thought it might make things too one-sided if he was allowed to play. It was probably a good choice. Herron, whose grandfather Lee played in the Ten Thousand Lakes tournament in the 1930s, played on the U.S. Walker Cup team in 1993 and would go on to compete on the PGA Tour, winning four tour events. Hoffman is now coaching Lumpy's sons, who are all very good junior golfers. 1997 would be the last time Orv's Invitational was held. Hagen moved to Las Vegas, where he passed away in 2002.

Like caddie master Lou Loomis, Orv was fond of betting on horses, dogs, and golfers. Orv's Invitational featured a pari-mutuel where people would bet on golfers to win, place, or show, similar to a horse or dog race. Cash was kept in a paper bag and the pari-mutuel tickets placed in an old cigar box kept behind the counter in the Traditional clubhouse. With no banks open on the weekend, Orv was known to have spent the night with $50,000 in the paper bag tucked under his bed for safekeeping.

Frank and Amy Cronin
"That's a peach, hon!"

Breezy Point's version of the Havercamps, Frank and Amy Cronin, came to Breezy and bought one of Billy Fawcett's cottages on the hill in 1963, after Frank retired as a Western Union manager in Cleveland, Ohio. A good golfer in his day, Frank was the starter at the Breezy Point Golf Course in the 1970s. Along with Ken Gilbert and Mac McChesney, Frank and Amy came up with the idea for a couple's scramble on Sunday afternoons. After playing with the Sunday

Couples League for years, the Cronins conceived the idea of a husband-and-wife tournament where each couple uses only one ball and alternates strokes on each hole until their ball reaches the hole. The Cronins donated a trophy for a tournament that became known as the "Divorce Open"!

Louise and Carl Martin, Breezy Point husband and wife champions in 1976 and 1977. Carl also wrote a poem about the Sunday Scramble back in the 1970s.

The Sunday Scramble by Carl Martin

When the season is over and the trees are all bare,
The wind's blowing strong and there's frost in the air.
The days grow shorter, alack and alas,
the snow will soon cover that beautiful grass.
Golfers have left to wherever they go, wanting to get away from
the ice and snow.
Well winter will come, and winter will go, then the sun will come
out and melt all the snow.
The days will get warmer, and the birds will all sing. All of sud-
den, by golly it's spring!
The golfers, who have been taking it easy, will all have the urge to
head back to Breezy.
There's Marlys and Fred, Doris and Don, and Orv and Alice too.
There's Carl and Louise and Susan and Keith, just to name a few.
The list gets longer every year, that's the way it should be
Cause that's how Dear Old Breezy gets it's Person-al-ity.
Two by Two they all come back and once more join the fold
Where tradition and good fellowship are more valuable than gold.
From now on we'll watch the weather, which sometimes can be
quite a gamble.
When the weekend comes and it doesn't rain, we'll have our Sun-
day Scramble.
And when we trod those fairways green, the ones we hold so
dear,
I hope we all say "Thank You God" for the start of another year!

—"Cronin Trophy"—

*Frank and Amy Cronin with 1980 husband-and-wife champions
Bev and Earle Wolley*

Father Ramacher

"Surely the Good Lord wouldn't ruin the best game of my life!"

Father Edward Ramacher takes the place of the golf-loving Bishop Pickering. Father Ramacher had a summer home on Lake Ossawinnamakee and played golf at Breezy Point for over 40 years. He and Don Heidt were frequent golf companions and occasionally would play with Bud Chapman when he was in the area visiting family. Chapman even included Father Ramacher and Heidt in one of his infamous golf hole paintings. The golf print is on display in the Traditional clubhouse and shows Ramacher in his customary knee-high stockings and khaki shorts.

I remember Father Rahmacher caddying for Heidt in the 1970 Billy Fawcett tournament. While Don hooked ball after ball into the woods on the back nine, the priest would go in like St. Anthony, the patron saint for the recovery of lost items, and find Heidt's ball every time!

Writing for the *Portland Oregonian* in February of 1920, Roscoe

Fawcett mentioned a pastor from St. Louis penning "An Epistle to Golfers," where he admitted that he, too, would play golf on Sunday morning if he were able to find time for "such a heavenly experience."

"However," he says, "there is such a thing as a golfer's religion. If he hasn't a religion, he needs one. It might help his game. Therefore, for those who spend the Sabbath forenoon on the links, the pastor has arranged a Saturday evening service."

Now spring forward to Breezy Point 50 years later. Tom Stanchfield and his wife enjoyed playing golf together at Breezy on Sunday mornings. That made it hard for them to make it to church, as there was no Saturday evening mass in the area at that time. Father Ramacher would arrange to come by the Stanchfield condo by the lake on Saturday and say mass in their home, using their bar as an altar. This would leave Sunday mornings open so Tom and his wife could play golf. Before long, the condo began filling up with people coming for mass on Saturdays, so Father was forced to put a stop to that!

Father Ramacher later lived in the Edgewater complex south of Breezy Point. By the early 2000s, he had stopped playing golf because of bad eyesight, unable to follow the ball in flight. He continued to enjoy his other passion, fishing, with his partner Marv Koep of Nisswa. Following the example of the disciples of Jesus, Father Ed was, above all, a fisher of men!

Loyal "Bud" Chapman

Bud Chapman is inextricably tied to the history of golf at Breezy Point. He started caddying at Interlachen Country Club in 1933 when he was 10 years old. He was a young Patty Berg's favorite caddie, earning 75 cents a round plus tips.

Fifty years later, Chapman qualified for the U.S. Senior Open at Hazeltine and played with Arnold Palmer. Bud won the Minnesota Senior Amateur in 1978 and 1990, as well as the Minnesota Senior Open in 1989. He is a member of the Minnesota Golf Hall of Fame.

Chapman is best known as the artist who created the 18 Infamous Golf Holes, each set alongside different geographical landmarks.

The first hole was created in the early 1970s, a par-3 across the Victoria Falls in Africa. There is another hole set on the edge of the Grand Canyon and a third that weaves its way through California's Redwood Forest.

Bud Chapman and his 54-inch driver at Whitebirch Golf Course in 1989. L-R Father Ramacher, Don Peddie, Bud Chapman, Breezy pro Dave Williams, Don Heidt, and course manager Orv Hagen.

Bud came to Breezy Point for a round of golf shortly after all 18 holes were opened at Whitebirch Golf Course in 1989. He shot a 78 from the back tees. Chapman also brought his camera along to shoot some pictures. There was talk of him doing a special-edition Infamous Golf Hole print based on one of Whitebirch's holes, possibly number 7, 16, or 17. Unfortunately, nothing ever came of that. It would have been interesting to see what he could have come up with.

Bud's mother was a resident at the Good Samaritan nursing home in Pine River. He would come up to visit her, fish, and play golf with brother-in-law Jack Dassett. Jack always included his friends Don Heidt and Father Edward Ramacher in their golf foursome. Chapman enjoyed using friends as models in his golf paintings, going into precise detail on their attire and giving them a quasi-cameo role in the play of one of his infamous golf holes.

For the 1991 U.S. Open program at Hazeltine, Chapman created four infamous Minnesota golf holes known as the "Nightmare Alley." If you look closely at the 175-yard par-3 15th hole at the fictitious Wild River Golf & Hiking Club, you'll see Don Heidt and Father Ramacher on the tee as their playing partner shoots for the green.

Bud was a tremendous golfer. He was a member of the Minneapolis Golf Club and Hazeltine National, carrying a plus-one handicap in his prime. Chapman won the Pine Beach tournament at Madden's Golf Course in 1949, 1960, and 1961, defeating favorite Kenny Young in the finals in 1949. He did not play very often in Breezy Point's Ten Thousand Lakes Tournament. His best finish here was a first-flight championship in 1957. In 1994, Bud used his 54-inch driver to beat an 18-year-old Tiger Woods in a long drive contest at the Porter Cup amateur tournament. Woods' drive was slightly longer but ended up in the rough so, as Chapman tells it, "Technically, I outdrove him!" Today, the USGA rules only allow a maximum driver length of 48 inches.

Don Heidt and Father Ramacher play one of Bud Chapman's infamous Minnesota golf holes!

My favorite Bud Chapman memory was watching him play in the 2015 MGA Senior Amateur held at Deacon's Lodge. A bit eccentric, Bud despised headcovers and golf bag zippers. He always kept the pockets in his golf bag open. Chapman's son Greg was the caddie responsible for not losing anything tucked away in the bag that day. In the second round of the tournament, Bud shot a 92, matching his age. In a lifetime of golf, he shot his age 3,899 times!

Bud kept track. From caddying for Patty Berg to playing golf against Arnold Palmer, and with a bit of history at each of Breezy Point's three golf courses, Bud Chapman has a well-deserved place in the history of golf at Breezy Point.

Chapter 9: The King is Coming

On August 11, 1992, the largest shopping mall on earth, the Mall of America, opened in suburban Minneapolis, ushering in a decade of peace, calm, and abundance. The bottomless goodwill known as "Minnesota Nice" transferred well to the resort industry in Northern Minnesota.

Championship golf courses sprang up all around the area. It was part of a 20-year period beginning in 1988 during which more than 3,500 golf courses were built in the United States. Golf was big again, and lots of people wanted in.

While development of the Pine Tree Golf and Country Club slowed to a halt as investors dropped out, Joe Doty unveiled plans to build a golf course just west of Breezy Point in 1993. His 18-hole Rice Lake Country Club would be a semi-private course topping out at 6,553 yards from the tips. A driving range was opened in 1993, but there were never enough investors/prospective members to get any work done on the golf course. The driving range land was eventually sold to the Pequot Lakes School District, and a new elementary school was built there in 2003.

Five miles west of Breezy Point, the city of Pequot Lakes didn't have to wait long for its own golf course. The Preserve golf course, designed by PGA Tour player Mike Morley, opened in 1996 to rave reviews and became part of the Grand View Lodge resort in 1997. The Classic at Madden's Resort on Gull Lake had its debut in the same year, and Cragun's on Gull Lake was planning to open two 18-hole Robert Trent Jones Jr. courses before the turn of the century.

Too much golf in one area? Pete Loyd didn't think so. While cross-country skiing in the Weaver Point area just north of Breezy Point in 1996, Loyd found the site for what would eventually be the area's preeminent golf course. The property had been sitting there since it was first discovered by the Pine Tree group in 1983. All Pete needed was money and a big name to design his golf course. Cue up Mel Brooks: "It's good to be the king!"

Arnie

Latrobe Country Club was a nine-hole course constructed in 1920 in the small industrial and mining town located 50 miles southeast of Pittsburgh. Milfred "Deke" Palmer was a member of the crew that built the course and would take on the position of course superintendent after it was completed. Deke's son Arnold grew up playing golf there and received instruction from his father, who was also a golf professional at the club. Deacon put Palmer's small hands on a cut-down golf club in the correct position and told him to never change his grip. Arnie never did. As a kid, he always played with a hand-me-down set of clubs. It is interesting to note a Breezy Point connection there. Palmer said his favorite clubs were a Walter Hagen driver and a Patty Berg brassie that stayed in his bag for many years.

Hagen's golf club company was purchased by Wilson Golf in 1944. The Haig Ultra irons became one of their signature lines for many years. Patty Berg signed a six-year contract with Wilson when she turned pro that lasted for 66 years! Palmer himself represented Wilson and played their equipment when he first turned pro.

The son of a greenskeeper, Arnie was involved in hands-on work as a young man, helping with maintenance at the golf course. In his sophomore year at Wake Forest College, he and some other members of the golf team used wheelbarrows and shovels to build the first grass greens on their nine-hole course, replacing the original sand greens. After joining the Coast Guard in 1951, Palmer was assigned to Camp May in New Jersey. The base commander asked Arnie to build a golf course there. He was given a rake, a shovel, and a hand-push mower and directed to a patch of grass between the airport runways. Doing all the mowing, shaping, and grooming, he put in a nine-hole chip-and-putt course that would be his first golf course design. Palmer later said, "Of all the courses I built, that one was probably not the most challenging layout, but certainly it was the most physically exhausting to create."

Additional land was purchased around Latrobe C.C. in the 1960s, and a second nine was added at that time. In 1963, Arnie took a break from the tour and came home to help his dad build the new nine, running a bulldozer to help shape the fairways and greens. Palmer purchased the club in 1971 and added some much-needed improvements to his home course. Today, Latrobe is a tight, rolling, and testing 6,500 yards with small greens and fairways lined with trees planted by Deke Palmer and his crew. Deacon still keeps an eye on his golf course. Some of the pine trees he planted in the early years were dying out. When the dead trees were removed, Arnold had an eight-foot stump saved from one of the trees along the 18th fairway. A chainsaw artist created a wooden statue of Deacon keeping an eye on each golfer as they come up the fairway to the final green.

Arnie got more involved in course design in 1969 when he

formed a partnership with Frank Duane, a disciple of Robert Trent Jones Sr. Duane and Palmer found inspiration for their design in the classic golf courses of golf's Golden Era. This included courses with the kind of layout that golfers of every skill level could appreciate and enjoy playing. He continued that philosophy when he teamed up with Ed Seay, who previously worked for Ellis Maples, in the early 1970s. Maples' father, Frank, had worked with Donald Ross at Pinehurst from 1907 to 1948. Palmer and Seay sealed their deal with a handshake. They would go on to form Palmer Golf Course Design in 1979 and worked together until Seay's death in 2007.

Ed Seay and Arnold Palmer take their first look at property in the Weaver Point area in 1997.

Along with Latrobe C.C., Palmer poured his heart and soul into one other golf course, a Dick Wilson design he found in Orlando, Florida, in the 1960s called the Bay Hill Club and Lodge. Bay Hill became the Palmers' winter home, a quiet retreat from the real world (at least until Disney World and Universal became next-door neighbors). Arnie took over the ownership of the Bay Hill Club and Lodge in 1975 and contracted with the PGA Tour in 1979 to host a golf tournament—the Arnold Palmer Invitational—during the tour's Florida swing in March. With the tour players there every year, Palmer would continue to make changes through the years to keep up with the young guns that showed up in March.

Finally, in 2009, Palmer Design performed a complete renovation of the course. Arnie wanted the course to play like a U.S. Open course off the tee, featuring thick rough and tight fairways that pointed toward the outer edges of bunkers, looped around inside, and continued to the outside of the greenside bunkers. Palmer also wanted the course to be like Augusta National around the greens, adding closely shaved slopes to give players a range of short-game options. The result was another classic design that was extremely challenging.

In one year alone in the 1990s, Palmer Design had almost 40 golf courses in various stages of completion. One of those projects would be his first golf course in Minnesota, and the only one that would carry his father's name.

Deacon Palmer: The Complex Relationships of Fathers and Sons

"The connection a man has with his father shapes his life. Which is why every adult son must choose how that relationship will or won't define him." –Joseph Hart from his article "Father and Son" in *Experience Life* magazine.

I was lucky. As an only child, I was able to receive my parents' undivided attention whenever I needed it. My father was a kind and gentle man who was always ready to help others who needed assistance. I cannot remember a music concert or sports contest I was involved in without my mother and father there watching. Today, when I see either of my sons being a good father, it reminds me of my dad. That is continuing a legacy!

Once a week, I take part in a program at our county jail called "Let's Talk." It is a chance for some of the men incarcerated there to get together and talk about what's going on in their lives. A common theme usually comes up, giving us a chance to see what the Bible has to say about loneliness, fear, anger, or whatever topic comes up that week. That leads to more conversation before we end with individual prayers for each of the guys. Let's Talk is always one of the highlights of my week.

One week, we talked about families, and I asked everyone to share a story about one of their siblings. There were lots of stories and lots of laughs that night! The next week, we shared a story about our mothers. There were both smiles and tears as the men talked about their mothers and/or grandmothers. It was another uplifting night.

I was eager to hear stories about their dads the following week, but I wasn't prepared for what came next. Stories of abuse, neglect, and abandonment went around the table. And then we got to the final inmate. At first, he didn't say anything. Then, after shaking his head back and forth a few times, he finally spoke up.

"My dad's a piece of crap!" he said. "I wish he was dead!"

Along with all the anger, frustration, and fear that came out that night, we also had a chance to talk about forgiveness and a heavenly father who loves us all unconditionally. Most of the men in jail were fathers themselves, separated from their families. It was a vicious cycle repeating itself over and over.

We left the men that night with an unanswered question: "Will that cycle ever be broken?" It was a powerful night, and incredibly eye-opening. When I think about the complex relationships of fathers and sons, I always remember that night in jail.

Milfred Jerome "Deacon" Palmer was born in 1904 and was a product of the Depression. As a teenager, he was one of the laborers who built the Latrobe Country Club in Latrobe, Pennsylvania. In 1926, he became the grounds superintendent, and in 1931 added the position of golf professional, selling equipment and giving lessons at the club. He was born with infantile paralysis and had a clubbed left foot. It caused him to walk with a limp. This led to teasing during his youth, which in turn led to fighting. Because of his physical impairment, the PGA refused to recognize him as a member of their organization until 1946.

As a young man, Palmer became involved in a common confrontation of that time. One day, he happened upon a scene where an African American church deacon was being harassed by a crowd of white people. Young Palmer stepped in and came to the man's rescue. Afterward, people began referring to him as "Deacon," and the name stuck. When asked about his nickname later in life, he would simply say, "I kept some other people from giving an old Black deacon a rough time."

Arnold Palmer used the words tough, hardworking, and honest to describe his father. "He stayed a tough guy all his life. He was tough on me," Palmer said.

Palmer's sister Lois recalls, "He was pretty hard on Arnold. I felt sorry for Arnie, but he wasn't hard on me. He left my problems up to my mother, and I was a good kid; I did all my schoolwork, and I was an A student. Poor Arnie had a rough time with schoolwork. He did more ordinary things than I ever did, so Daddy was tough on him."

About his father, Arnold said, "He was sort of a buddy, but I was scared of him, and I was scared because he was tough, and he didn't take a lot of sass or anything from me. He told me what to do and I did it as fast as I could get it done. That included playing golf."

Palmer received affection from his mother, Doris, a friendly woman with a gentle spirit. He always appreciated that even as he desperately sought his father's acceptance. Arnold's daughter Amy described his relationship with Deacon as loving but volatile. Palmer spent his life trying to make his dad proud by being aggressive, winning tournaments, capturing majors, making money, and building a name brand.

Daughter Peggy said, "I think that he absolutely wanted to prove himself to his father."

After winning the US Amateur in 1954, Deacon told his son, "You did pretty good, boy." In his autobiography, *A Golfer's Life*, Arnie recalls "This meant the world to me, and I felt my own tears coming. I'd finally shown my father that I was the best amateur golfer in America. It was the turning point of my life, and I don't know if I have ever felt as much happiness on a golf course."

Neil Chethik, the author of *Fatherloss*, reminds sons that "when we are not reconciled with our fathers, there is something inside of us that remains restless, and there's also something that remains kidlike. We don't really grow up until we have come to terms with our fathers. We need our fathers to bless us in a way that brings us into adulthood…For most men, earning their father's acceptance has a profound effect on their relationships and their self-image. There is something about the words 'I'm proud of you' coming from a father that cannot be duplicated and clears away any wreckage in the relationship."

Golf Channel's Managing Editor, Mercer Baggs, brought the subject up in a conversation with Arnold Palmer on his 85th birthday in 2014. In his article "Arnie Palmer's Father, an imposing, lasting figure," he wrote: *Arnold Daniel Palmer is not the same man as Milfred Jerome Palmer. But Arnie is who he is because of Deacon. Complex relationships, fathers and sons. But Arnold must know, even without verbal authority, he has to know Deacon was proud of what his boy accomplished, and he did love his son. His son has to know that. Right? "Well," today's Mr. Palmer says, noticeably uncomfortable to be delving this personally, "I suppose I do."*

Deacon's Lodge Golf Course

The only course in the Palmer Design Company's portfolio named after Arnie's father, Deacon's Lodge Golf Course in Breezy Point would undoubtedly meet with Deacon Palmer's approval if he were alive today. The 495-acre site includes three lakes and several deep wilderness wetlands on a 170-foot layer of glacial sand. Norway and white pines, birch, oak, basswood, and aspen trees are found throughout a property that offers several elevation changes providing stunning views throughout the golf course. By using the entire 495 acres, each hole has its own identity and space. Very few houses are within sight of the course. Designed to be environmentally friendly, the golf course does not infringe on any wetlands or lakes. It is a shining jewel in the north woods. And it was almost an afterthought!

In 1983, an organization called the Ten Group acquired the land where Deacon's Lodge sits and came up with a plan to develop the Pine Tree Golf and Country Club. Designed by architect Bill Kubly of Lincoln, Nebraska, Pine Tree Golf and Country Club was conceived as an 18-hole golf course that would include approximately 250 homesites nestled among the golf holes. With part of the land being in the city of Breezy Point and part of the land in Pelican Township, the developers had to deal with both city and county government planning and zoning committees. An Environmental Assessment Worksheet was completed in December of 1983 with an Environmental Impact Statement forthcoming in March of 1984. The city of Breezy Point gave the project conditional approval if they would connect the homesites to the city sewer system. Crow Wing County Planning and Zoning did not approve the Environmental Impact Statement, and the project was put on hold pending a lawsuit filed against the county by the group, now known as the Midwest Fifteen.

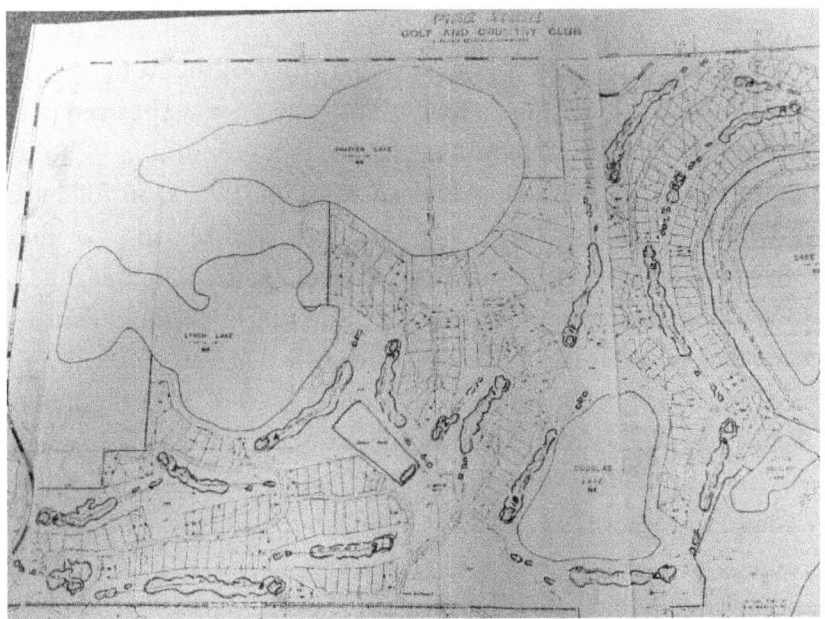

*The design for Pine Tree Golf and Country Club. Routing done by
Bill Kubly of Landscapes, Unlimited. October 31, 1983.*

The project started up again in 1989, only to encounter re-
sistance from two groups: the Crow Wing Environmental Protection Association and the Pelican Lakes Property Owners Association. Attorney Peter Bachman voiced the two groups' concern that
concept approval was granted by the city without any development
plans, with no projected densities, with no layout, without knowing
which wetlands would be filled, and without evaluating the effects
of the development on the environment. They also wanted to see
a market and feasibility study done on the property. In October
1990, Midwest Fifteen spokesperson John Finley stated that two
of the investors were now dead and two more were in bankruptcy.
The project was put on hold again.

In August of 1995, Don Peddie reported in the *Lake Country*

Echo that one of the Midwest Fifteen investors had arranged an onsite visit to the property by a representative of the Robert Trent Jones golf course design company. The visitor was impressed with the site. Peddie speculated there was enough ground for 18 holes, plus 100 or more residential lots. In April of 1996, Don followed up with a report that "there is now activity with regard to ownership of the site. The property is for sale and attracting interest."

While in Minnesota for the Senior Burnet Classic Golf Tournament that summer, Arnold Palmer was asked about the chance of a Palmer Design course in Minnesota someday. He responded, "Right now we're doing work for Minnesota people in other states, and maybe we'll get lucky here too." Palmer was referring to the Sienna Corporation's Tradition Golf Club in La Quinta, California. The course was a Palmer Design built by Landscapes, Unlimited out of Lincoln, Nebraska. Landscapes Unlimited had built 20 other Palmer courses and was owned by Bill Kubly, the same person who had done the course design for the Pine Tree Golf and C.C. Small world, indeed.

Sienna World Golf acquired the site in 1997 and contracted with the Arnold Palmer Design Company to create a golf course with a limited number of homesites attached. Erik Larsen of Palmer Design was the lead architect for the project. A native of Newton, Iowa, Larsen had a degree in landscape architecture from North Carolina State University and started working with the Palmer company in 1983. He worked there for 28 years before starting his own company, Larsen Golf, in 2011. Erik is a past president of the American Society of Golf Course Architects and has designed over 100 golf courses in a career that now spans 38 years. Larsen recalled that the smallest site Palmer Design ever worked on was at the Mill Cove Golf Course in Florida. There were less than 100 acres available to put an 18-hole course on. Deacon's

Lodge gave them almost five times the acreage they had available at Mill Cove. The rolling terrain, sand-based soil, and inherent natural beauty were an ideal site for a golf course. Best of all, there was no housing development they had to work around. Larsen told me, "Deacon's was a special one!"

Arnold Palmer set the basic design philosophy for his courses and gave his architects the freedom to work within those parameters. Palmer drew his inspiration from the classic courses of America's golden age of design. He liked the classically shaped layouts that golfers of every level could appreciate and enjoy playing. Erik said his marching orders were to 1) keep the features visible, 2) place greens on the edge of features, and 3) always remember you are spending someone else's money!

Palmer's partner in design, Ed Seay, was an ex-Marine who was more hands-on regarding the design. Larsen describes Seay as a people person unlike any he has met. "He always tried to provide fun courses for all players. Ed was exceptionally practical in getting the golf course built and did not tolerate complications created by people with frivolous concerns. He liked to get on with it, and usually did."

It should be noted that Deacon's Lodge was finished a month ahead of schedule. Seay liked to clear his golf holes a little wider to give more room for the dirt work. Golfers at Deacon's can thank him for the 45- to 75-yard-wide fairways they get to play to from the tee.

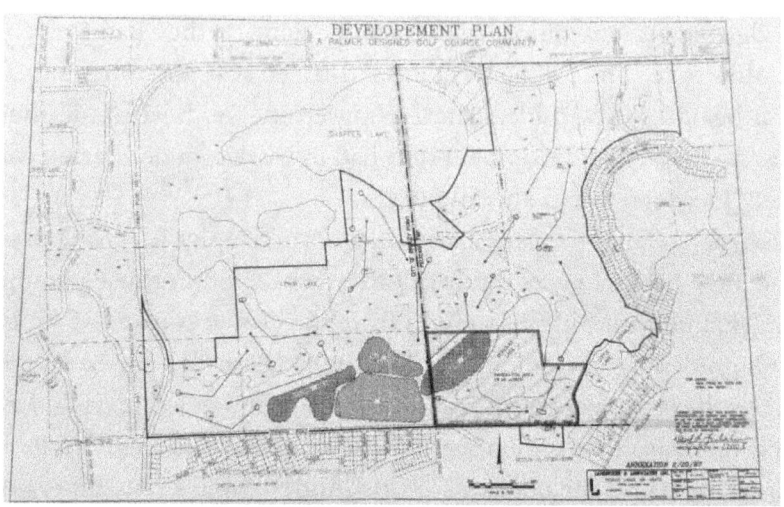

The original routing plan for Deacon's Lodge GC in early 1997. Hole 6 is in a different place, and Hole 8 is a sharp dogleg left. The back nine has most of the holes further to the east, with holes 16 and 17 on the east side of Douglas Lake and Hole 18, a par-4, running east to west, directly into the setting sun.

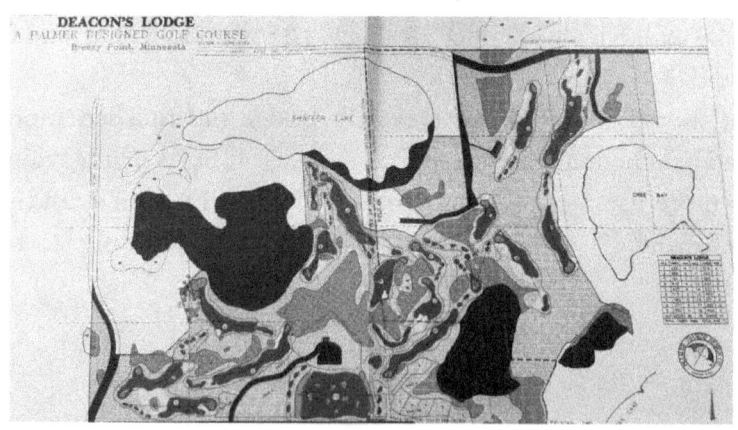

The final revision of Deacon's Lodge GC dated June 8, 1998. This is the course as you would find it today.

Bradley Klein, in his book on golf course design *Rough Meditations*, wrote: *The most important element in planning a golf course is the routing of the holes. The basic routing only works when it includes a thorough incorporation of wetlands, construction contours, available sunlight, drainage patterns, shot-making balance, and an internal rhythm to the succession of holes.*

Erik Larsen's strong point has always been in the routing of a golf course. He likes to do the mapping first and then clear a 10-yard width on each hole for a sight line as he begins to walk the course and shape the design of each hole. He credits Pete Dye with his concept of placing features on alternating sides of a hole when possible. It gives the average golfer room to play safe but requires the better player to aim close to the trouble to get a better angle and an easier shot into the green.

Larsen did a wonderful job at Deacon's Lodge of using the rolling terrain to contain the player's ball in the fairway and around the green. The starters at the course will advise golfers to play their ball to the high side of the fairway to let the ground help them and have an easier shot into the green. There is, however, always more than one way to play any hole at Deacon's.

Erik's design creed is "variety creates interest and interest creates fun." Hole 7 is an excellent example of that philosophy. Larsen created a second green alongside the wetland area to the right of the dogleg right fairway. When the forward green was in play, golfers had the option of playing directly at the green or laying up safely to the left. The first hole-in-one at Deacon's Lodge was made by Bart Taylor of Crosslake, Minnesota, on Hole 7 from the Deacon tees playing to the forward green—330 yards with his driver in one shot! Variety creates interest, interest creates fun, and sometimes the result can be a hole-in-one!

Golf course architect Erik Larsen

PGA professional Brad Brewer had this to say about his friend Erik Larsen: "He is a master at what he does, and I have always admired the creativity and attention to detail to create an amazing golf course; a course that remains playable for all, environmentally sensitive, and natural in its completion." Brewer was not talking about Deacon's Lodge, but if you've had a chance to play there, you can attest to the fact that Erik checked all those boxes when Deacon's was finished.

Enebak Construction of Lakeville, Minnesota, served as the builder at Deacon's, with Sienna World Golf's project manager, Pete Loyd, and course superintendent, Scott Schunter, also on-site during the construction process. Architect Erik Larsen wanted to give special notice to Jim Felton, the lead shaper, for his attention to detail in forming the land as close as possible to what was drawn up on paper. The construction involved clearing and grubbing 125 acres, moving 110,000 cubic yards of earth, installing 35,000 linear feet of asphalt paths, and setting up a 960-head Rain Bird automatic irrigation system powered by a 1,500-gallon-per-minute P&H pump station. When finished, the course included 134,000 square feet of putting green surface, 289,000 square feet of finished tee area, 45 acres of bent grass fairway, 30 acres of fescue rough, 12 acres of waste bunker, fairways with a width of 45 to 75 yards, and an 18-acre driving range featuring 350 linear yards of tee area on both ends.

Scott Shunter, Jim Felton, Pete Loyd, and Erik Larsen

Pete Loyd first came to the area as a minority partner in the Preserve Golf Course at Pequot Lakes, where he ran a bulldozer and received an education in golf course construction. A former golf professional, Loyd had worked for Control Data for several years before the "golf itch" returned and turned his life in a different direction. While cross-country skiing in the Weaver Point area in 1996, Pete stood at the top of the hill overlooking what would become the 17th hole at Deacon's Lodge and decided this might be a good place to build a golf course. He put together a group of investors who were friends from North Dakota but soon found out the project was too big for his group. John Hankinson and the Sienna Corporation came on board along with Tip Enebak of Enebak Construction, and the project began to move forward. The 495-acre Pine Tree Golf tract was purchased from the remaining members of the Midwest Fifteen, and Arnold Palmer Design was hired to map out the golf course. It would be the first Arnold Palmer golf course in Minnesota.

As the project manager, Loyd's first task would be working with the environmental groups that shut down the Pine Tree project. Pete adopted a cooperative rather than an adversarial relationship with the city, county, and environmental groups involved. A committee was formed to monitor the golf course development, and regular meetings were held where Loyd reported on construction progress and took the committee on a tour of the project so they could see the measures being taken to protect and preserve the natural state of the area. Suggestions from the committee were welcomed. Whenever possible, natural areas were left undisturbed. The Palmer design did not require a lot of earth moving, leaving a very natural look when the course was completed. Pete remembers the beautiful 17th green site looking the same today as it did when he looked out at it on skis in 1996.

Deacon's first course superintendent, Scott Schunter, was a native of DeWitt, Iowa, with a B.S. in horticultural science from Iowa State University. Scott was a foreman at Blackwolf Run GC in 1989 before becoming an assistant superintendent at Hazeltine National, where he supervised crews and helped prepare the course for the 1991 U.S. Open. From 1994 to 1997, Schunter assisted in the construction and maintenance of Jack Nicklaus' Bearpath Golf Course in Edina. Scott officially became the superintendent at

Deacon's Lodge in the spring of 1998, but unofficially he had been on site since the fall of 1997 when construction started. He was involved in the clearing and grubbing and helped with the shaping as well as the irrigation design.

The 17th hole at Deacon's Lodge, named one of the King's Dream 18 holes

Schunter's work in developing both Blackwolf Run and Bearpath was a big help at Deacon's Lodge. Scott commented that the sand-based soil made some things easier and other things more difficult. The pure sand base made it easier to clear the trees and brush and then shape the sand. With the excellent drainage in the sand, it was also easy to shape and install the irrigation without delays. The seeding process was more difficult. It was harder to move around in the sand with the tractors and seeders.

Deacon's current course superintendent, Ed Thomas, was also a member of the construction team. Ed remembers two heavy rains that lasted for several weeks in June of 1998, causing major washouts and requiring reseeding of some holes three or four times. Despite the rain delays, the course was finished a month ahead of schedule in the spring of 1999.

The two pictures on the next page show the fifth hole at Deacon's Lodge during the clearing and shaping process, and again after the growing-in process and several years of maturation. Notice the minimal amount of earth moved and the protective area preserved between Lynch Lake and the golf hole.

At first glance, Deacon's Lodge reminds golfers of Pine Valley, one example of the classic courses Palmer admired. Two forced carries on the opening hole, waste bunkers scattered throughout the course, and a nasty bunker fronting the 11th hole (like the one on Pine Valley's 10th hole, named after a part of the devil's anatomy, which we'll not discuss here) all shout Pine Valley to the golfer. However, if the golfer listens to the starter on the first tee and plays to the high side of the fairway, he finds he can maneuver his ball around the wetlands on the first hole and avoid the forced carry. Sometimes the ground will repel your shot away from the green, while at other times, it will carry the ball toward the green. Instead of Pine Valley, you're now moving your ball along the ground, similar to links golf in Scotland. If you miss a green at Deacon's, you can find yourself looking up at the pin from one of the many chipping areas alongside some greens. Now you're at Pinehurst and must decide if you'll fly your ball to the pin with a wedge or roll it up with a putter. Or a hybrid. Or… Every shot at Deacon's can leave you with choices. Variety creates interest, and interest creates fun.

Hole Number 5 at Deacon's Lodge during construction
(Photo by Ed Thomas)

Hole Number 5 at Deacon's Lodge completed

On May 31, 1999, Palmer, Seay, and lead architect Erik Larsen arrived at the only Palmer design named after Arnie's father for the grand opening of Deacon's Lodge Golf Course. Three hundred and fifty invited guests were on hand to watch Palmer and Minnesota Governor Jesse Ventura play the course. It was my first day on the job as a Deacon's employee, as I would be one of the men holding a rope around the tee while Arnie and Jesse hit their drives. On my way to the first tee, I ran into Ed Seay. When I inquired about a good time to ask for an autograph, the ex-Marine officer straightened up. Looking directly into my eyes, he said, "After the round is over, Mr. Palmer will sign anything." On to the first hole.

The governor and the general

They would be playing only the back nine today due to some unseasonably cold weather, so along with my new friends Jim and

Terry, I went to the tenth tee to set up our rope. Soon, the general of Arnie's Army and the ex-Navy Seal governor arrived at the tee. After posing for pictures, it was time for the opening tee shots. Governor Ventura's first drive went out of play. I remember Palmer telling him, "Hit 'til you're happy, Governor." A sleeve of Titleist Professionals later, Jesse finally had one in play. Arnie's first swing was a bullet right down the middle.

As the two golfers hit their approach shots into the 12th green, Pete Loyd, project manager for Deacon's, asked us to go ahead to the 13th tee and move the markers up. Playing from the tips, the 450-yard hole was playing dead into a cold north wind that would make it play like a three-shot par 5.

We moved the markers up a tee box and waited. When Palmer arrived, he stood on the back tee, looked around, and asked us where the markers were. After telling him we'd moved them up, he pointed down at the ground by his feet and said, "Put 'em back here." Arnie then proceeded to stripe another drive followed by a 3-wood he laced onto the green 30 feet from the pin. Not bad for a 70-year-old golfer!

I didn't see the finish of Hole 13 as we had to travel quite a distance through the woods to get set up on the 14th tee. Palmer got a ride on a golf cart and reached the tee about the same time we did. The rest of the gallery was walking and would not show up for a few minutes. I convinced Jim to give me the small camera he'd brought along so I could take his picture with Arnie. After taking the picture, I said, "Now, Jim, come here and take my picture with Mr. Palmer."

Terry also got his picture with the king. We must have been Arnie's good-luck charm, as he hit a nice wedge to 15 feet on the par 5 and made the putt for his only birdie of the day.

The author and Arnold Palmer, opening day at
Deacon's Lodge

He could have used some of that good luck on the next hole. Arnie's drive on 15 went low and left and didn't make it across the large waste bunker in front of the tee. It was his only bad shot of the round. Turning to the crowd with a smirk on his face, he said, "That looked like one of Winnie's drives!" The crowd chuckled as Palmer teed up another ball and spanked it right down the middle. Seven pars with the birdie on 14 and a bogey on 15 would give Palmer an even par score for his round on the course named after his father.

When Arnie stepped on the tee of the par-3 17th hole, he looked out at the island green 200 yards away surrounded by wetlands, whistled softly, and said, "Oh, this is *purrty*!" When he made a list of the Dream 18 holes created by Palmer Design in 2005, number 17 at Deacon's Lodge GC was on that list. Look for a big rock behind the 17ᵗʰ tee with a plaque commemorating that honor if you ever play golf at Deacon's.

After putting out on the 18ᵗʰ green, Palmer walked off to the side where I was standing. I was ready with a black Sharpie marker, a brand-new Deacon's Lodge golf cap, and my copy of Palmer's biography, *A Golfer's Life*. Grabbing the pen I held in my hand, he signed the bill of the cap and the inside cover of the book with the same impeccable penmanship he had used a million times before. As we retired to the large tent set up in the parking lot for food and drinks, I noticed Arnie had time for everyone who came up to greet him. Each of the 350 guests got their moment with the king, and he had a way of making everyone feel like they were with their new best friend.

Arnie, on behalf of all your many fans, "Thanks for the memories!"

Governor Ventura grabbed a quick bite to eat and decided to brave the cold and play another nine. Wearing just a short-sleeved Deacon's Lodge polo shirt, Jesse made a quick trip around the front nine. When he finished, he had this to say about his day: "Mr. Palmer is so gracious to everybody. He is a great lesson on how to live your life. This area will prosper tremendously from Deacon's Lodge."

Deacon's Lodge has received many honors including *Golf Digest*'s "America's 100 Greatest Public Courses," *Golf Magazine*'s "Top 100 Courses You Can Play," and *Links Magazine*'s "#2 Best Arnold Palmer Design in the World."

On Arnold Palmer's 85th birthday, Golf Channel travel guide Matt Ginella ranked the top Arnold Palmer-designed courses that are available for public play. The Bay Hill Club and Lodge was ranked first, Turtle Bay Resort in Hawaii was second, and Deacon's Lodge was the third best design, in Ginella's opinion.

I related that story to a Taylor Made representative as he was getting ready to tee off at Deacon's Lodge a few years ago. He said, "I've played Turtle Bay, this is better." When I mentioned Bay Hill, he replied, "I've played there too. This course is just as good."

Arnold Palmer Design created over 300 golf courses during Palmer's lifetime. The list of courses is impressive, and opinions will vary on where Deacon's Lodge ranks on the list. I do know from watching Arnie play at the course opening in 1999 that he was proud of the finished product. And, if Deacon Palmer had been around, I think he would have looked out at the course bearing his name and said, "You did pretty good, boy!"

Hit 'Til You're Happy, Governor

Canadian golfer David Bernard Mulligan is credited with inventing the golf mulligan back in the 1920s. Here is his story, told in a 1952 interview with Don Mackintosh of the *Sudbury Star*.

One day while playing in my usual foursome, I hit a ball off the first tee that was long enough but not straight. I was so provoked with myself that on impulse I stooped over and put another ball down. The other three looked at me with considerable puzzlement and one of them asked, "What are you do-ing?" "I'm taking a correction shot," I replied. "What do you call that?" the partner inquired. Thinking fast, I told him that I called it a "mulligan". After that it became kind of an unwritten rule in our foursome that you could take an extra free shot on the first tee if you weren't satisfied with the original. Naturally, this always was referred to as "taking a mulligan."

KFAN radio's Dan "Common Man" Cole loves to play golf (and talk about it on KFAN radio). Common was proclaimed the Official Unofficial Ambassador for Minnesota Golf by Governor Jesse Ventura in 2001. He does a radio show annually at Deacon's Lodge when he makes a golf trip up north and loves to play the course whenever possible. Cole has his own version of the mulligan: If the first hole does not go as planned, Cole will go back and replay the entire hole…if the course isn't busy. Cole refers to it as a "restart." My sons refer to it as "taking a Common."

On May 30, 1999, Arnold Palmer and Governor Ventura approached the 10th tee at Deacon's Lodge for their first tee shot in the ceremonial course opening. Each golfer had a brand-new box of Titleist Professional golf balls in their bag, courtesy of head pro Mark Neva.

After slicing his first tee shot into the trees, Ventura heard Arnie say, "Hit 'til you're happy, Governor." A sleeve of balls later, Jesse put one in the fairway. It was the first of several mulligans or "breakfast balls" we saw throughout their round. Even Palmer had his turn. On the long par-four 15th hole, Arnie's drive went low and left, failing to clear the waste bunker in front of the tee. With a smile on his face, Palmer looked at the gallery and said, "That looked like one of Winnie's drives." While we chuckled at that, he teed up another ball and stripped it right down the middle.

Ventura is not the only governor who has played golf at Breezy Point. Lt. Governor Louis Collins hit the opening tee shot at the first Ten Thousand Lakes Tournament in 1924. Governor J.A.O. Preus also played golf at Chippewa Links with Billy and Roscoe Fawcett while vacationing at Breezy Point with his family in 1924.

Floyd Olson played in the Ten Thousand Lakes Tournament when he was a Hennepin County attorney and continued to visit Breezy and play golf after he was elected governor in 1930. A member of the Minneapolis Golf Club, Olson recorded a net-74 at the Breezy Small Ball Tournament held over the Fourth of July in 1931 and won the long-drive contest with a shot of 310 yards! His wife, Ada, was also an excellent golfer who won the Ladies' Championship at the Pine Beach tournament in 1935. Olson had a summer home on Gull Lake and was a regular at Breezy Point in the 1920s and 30s. In the midst of the Prohibition Era, he enjoyed the party-like atmosphere at Breezy.

Minnesota governor Karl Rolvaag visited Breezy shortly after becoming governor in 1963. Here we see him checking out golf equipment at the new Breezy Point pro shop with pro Max Evans and owner Don Eastvold looking on. Eastvold and Rolvaag were classmates at St. Olaf College in the 1950s.

Undoubtably the best athlete among Minnesota's governors was Wendell Anderson, who was a member of the 1956 silver medal U.S. Olympic hockey team coached by John Mariucci. A University of Minnesota athlete, Anderson played in the celebrity golf tournament at Breezy in 1976. The picture below shows Anderson with partners Frank Fitzsimmond, Gene Wilson, and Father Rahmacher.

In the 1930s, Harry Truman, a colonel in the Army Reserves, would train at Fort Ripley. This put him near one of his favorite spots, Breezy Point. Harry liked to play the slots and was known to hit the jackpot a time or two while visiting Breezy. Truman went on to serve as a U.S. senator from Missouri, as Franklin Roosevelt's vice president, and then as president of the United States from 1945 to 1952.

Minnesota governors Harold LaVander, Rudy Perpich, and Tim Pawlenty have all been to Breezy Point for the Governor's Fishing Opener. The only golfer in the group, Pawlenty has been back to play golf at Deacon's Lodge several times since leaving office. Like the rest of us, Tim has been known to take an extra shot off the first tee when necessary. As Arnold Palmer would have said, "Hit 'til you're happy, Governor!"

Elvis: 980 Miles from Graceland

Once the playground of Captain Billy Fawcett's friends from Hollywood, Breezy Point today features performances by musical giants Elvis Presley, Johnny Cash, and Neil Diamond during the summer season. 980 miles from Graceland, Elvis impersonator Chris Olson calls Breezy Point his summer home. You can find him at Dockside on Saturday nights performing his two-hour Memories of Elvis tribute show. He has been a featured performer here at Breezy Point for the last 31 years. Hundreds of golfers, locals, weekenders, vacationers, and time-sharers make up the crowd filling up the picnic tables, lawn chairs, and pontoon boats that are pulled up along the beach. The voice is pure Elvis as Chris sings and gyrates onstage. The appreciative crowd applauds and always shouts for more.

Elvis Presley was an occasional golfer who enjoyed playing golf whenever his schedule allowed. He was known to use a Harley Davidson golf cart to move around his property at Graceland. Many times, Presley would have to wear a straw hat and a fake beard as a disguise when he played golf to avoid being recognized by his many fans. One time, while playing with legendary golfer Gary Player, he asked Mr. Player for some help with his golf swing. Player said, "In the golf swing, you have to use the hips." Elvis replied, "You're talking to the right man!"

Chris describes himself as a bogey golfer who plays about once a week during the golf season. He was introduced to the game when he was younger during physical education class at school but didn't have an actual golf lesson until he was in his 30s. He likes to play in the Monday afternoon scramble at the Traditional Golf Course and never misses the Charlie's Scramble at Whitebirch Golf Course on the first Tuesday of the month. Olson always plays with his stepson, Nick, and will rotate several friends to fill out their threesome. His favorite Charlie's memory is the steak dinner after the round, always cooked to perfection by chef Dave Gravdahl. He also mentioned his drive one year on the 324-yard 16th hole that ended up on the fringe of the green. Not bad for a bogey golfer! Chris told me his lowest golf score was a 77 shot at the Tara Golf and Country Club in Bradenton, Florida, where he spends the winter months.

Olson's favorite course in the Breezy rotation is Deacon's Lodge. He remembers being asked to perform at a party thrown there by Sienna World Golf when the course first opened. Olson really enjoys the Palmer Design course and makes a point of playing there whenever time allows. He does not order an Arnold Palmer as his beverage of choice, but he does enjoy an Elvis Presley: A sandwich consisting of peanut butter, banana, and bacon on toasted bread. He's hoping Breezy Point might add that to their menu one of these days!

True icons are people usually known only on a first-name basis. Arnie and Elvis are two such icons. In Brad Brewer's book on Arnold Palmer, *Mentored by the King*, Palmer mentioned that he never really cared for the nickname "The King" as it made him feel uncomfortable and a bit irritated at times. It is purely with affection that we refer to those two giants here by that moniker. Only at Breezy Point can you play a golf course designed by a king during the day and listen to another king perform for you at night. Throw in lunch with an Elvis Presley sandwich and an Arnold Palmer drink, and you'll have had a special day. At Breezy Point, that's about as good as it gets!

Even Elvis likes to play golf at Breezy Point!

Chapter 10: The New Millenium

The beginning of the 21st century was littered with recessions, stock market crashes, and flat-out disasters all around—most notably, the September 11, 2001, attack on the World Trade Towers in New York City. Shock, sadness, fear, and anger were among the many feelings Americans expressed in response to the attack. Everyone now became more cautious and concerned about life in their country. The stock market dropped quickly after the 9-11 attack, and most businesses felt the hit. The U.S. economy was already going through a small recession following the dot-com bubble. Most areas recovered quickly, but steep declines hit the travel, tourism, hospitality, and entertainment industries, all of which impacted the growth of golf. Between 2003 and 2018, golf saw a decline of over 6.8 million players with more than 1,200 golf courses closing their doors. For a time, Deacon's Lodge looked like it might become one of those courses.

Opening in 1999, Deacon's Lodge was owned by Sienna World Golf and managed by Grand View Lodge for 14 years. When the bottom fell out of the housing market in the late 2000s, Sienna was forced to put the golf course up for sale. It was purchased by Whitebirch, Inc., the parent company of Breezy Point, in November 2012. Breezy's owner, Bob Spizzo, remembers being at the golf

241

course opening when Arnold Palmer played in 1999. Admiring the new golf course, he turned to his grandson and said, "Someday, I'm going to own this."

That day had arrived. The purchase gave Breezy Point a world-class Arnold Palmer-designed course to add to a rotation of what is now 54 holes of golf. Breezy has been a good steward of the land and the golf course since taking over in 2013. One of their first moves was retaining the services of head pro Mark Neva and course superintendent Ed Thomas. PGA professional Mark Neva has been the head pro at Deacon's from the beginning. Mark has overseen getting the golf course up and running since day one and remains a key player in its success over the last 26 years. Neva remembers looking at the course for the first time in the winter. Even with snow on the ground, he could tell he was looking at something special.

"It was dramatically impressive at first sight. You could see its potential," he said. Mark always gives credit to his staff for helping to make Deacon's Lodge a great place to work and play golf. Some have been with him for all 26 years, but special notice must go to superintendent Ed Thomas, who has been working at Deacon's since construction began at the course in 1997. It's safe to say he knows every inch of the 495 acres the course sits on. Ed has a hard-working staff, and everyone takes pride in keeping the course that Arnie built in great condition.

Breezy Point's other two courses survived the golf recession as well, thanks in part to improvements made over the years. Additional bunkering was added at Whitebirch GC in the fall of 1998 under the direction of Pete Loyd of Sienna World Golf. Pete was also working on the bunker design at Deacon's Lodge Golf Course during this time. Whitebirch added 14 new standard-type bunkers and nine waste bunkers. With tall grass around them, the waste bunkers added a little Scottish flavor to the course and helped collect golf balls that might otherwise have found their way into the woods.

Designer Loyd said, "Our objective was to be as little disruptive as possible to the playing strengths of the course but to maximize a changed look and a feeling of greater playability. We strove to add definition and distance perspective when indicated. The waste bunkers are large and will become a distinctive feature of the golf course."

Hole Number 6 received a waste bunker on the left side, a fairway bunker, and a large bunker behind the green to give it a different appearance and much better definition. Loyd was especially pleased about the changes to the 16th hole, a dogleg par-four around a huge wetlands area. A waste bunker was added along the landing area on the left side, as well as new fairway bunkers at critical distances from the tee. The changes give the hole the appearance of a Cape hole in a dramatic, natural setting. General Manager Dave Gravdahl added that "Breezy Point was the first in the Lake Country area to introduce a championship-length golf course. Now we are taking the steps to complete that process."

In 2003, a significant design change was made to Hole Number 7, with a new back tee added that stretched the par five to 550 yards. The water hazard on the right side, overgrown with weeds, was cleaned out as well. A new Toro automatic sprinkler system was installed throughout the course, ensuring that all the fairway areas and much of the rough could now be watered regularly. In 2010, the 10th hole was shifted to the left, with a new green added to make room for a series of townhomes on the right side of the hole. In recent years, Breezy Point has consulted with former Madden's Golf Course superintendent and golf architect Scott Hoffmann on plans to continue upgrading and improving the course.

Hole Number 7 new tee and water hazard cleaned up in 2003

Hoffmann added a waste bunker and mounds on Hole 11 to realign the hole and create a buffer for the new condominium development on the right. Plans are also in place for a redesign of Holes 8 and 9, which will eliminate a blind tee shot and open up both holes. Scott's main emphasis was on turfgrass maintenance, particularly eliminating the poa annua grass in the greens and bringing out the preferred bent grass found on better-putting surfaces.

The back nine at Whitebirch features a memorable sequence of holes. The many elevation changes on the course come into play on the 15th hole, a 502-yard par-five. The golfer tees off into a valley with a large hump in the middle. From the valley, the golfer must play back up to a green sitting at the top of a steep hill.

Whitebirch Number 15, looking back from the green at the twists and slopes in the fairway

The 16th hole is a dogleg right par-four. It curves around the wetlands where ducks, geese, and a beaver hut give the golfer a little taste of Northern Minnesota. The par-3 17th hole plays 205 yards over water from the back tee and features a rock-framed water cascade on the left side of a large, well-sloped green. Hole 18 added new tees closer to the highway that requires tee shots to start out across a small pond before following an uphill dogleg left fairway to the green.

Whitebirch Hole 17

The Breezy 54

In his autobiography, *The Walter Hagen Story*, Sir Walter writes about playing three golf courses in one day while preparing for the 1920 British Open: *Anyone who knows the coastal links in Kent County, southeast of London, will remember there are three links adjoining each other. Deal, the first, Sandwich directly east, known as the Royal St. George's, then a little south of Sandwich and east lies the Prince's links. While we were in London for the 1920 British Open, Jim Barnes and I started one morning to play the three links as if they were one. After playing eleven holes on the Deal course, we hopped a fence over to Sandwich and played ten holes there, crossed to the Prince's links and completed all the holes there, coming back to the original starting place. We finished the remainder of the holes on the Sandwich and Deal layouts, ending up on the eighteenth at Deal. Scores? I've forgotten. We weren't trying to break any records. We were lucky to go that far. We did it for fun.*

In the spirit of the Haig, we decided to play all three golf courses at Breezy Point on the Fourth of July in 2020. With temperatures up in the 90s that day, we were only able to complete 18 holes before having to retire inside to escape the sweltering heat. Not to be dissuaded, we came back the second week in August to give it one more try. We didn't have as much daylight to work with, but an early tee time at Whitebirch GC got us off to a flying start.

We slid into an open tee time around noon at Deacon's Lodge and made good time on a busy day there. Getting to the Traditional course around 4:30, we found the men's league beginning a shot-gun start on the front nine. Since they were only playing nine holes, we started on the back nine and played a three-man scramble. The front nine was open as we made the turn, so we were able to continue play on the front and finished before dark.

Unlike Hagen, the Aulies always keep score! We had a best ball score of 67 at Whitebirch, where Grandpa was the medalist with a 75. Son Marcus was the medalist at Deacon's with a 77, and we made six birdies to shoot a best ball 66. At the Traditional, we had a putt on our last hole for a 59 but missed it and had to settle for a scramble score of 60. Like Walter Hagen, we did it for fun and thoroughly enjoyed ourselves!

In 1992, basketball GOAT, Michael Jordan, was in Orlando for the NBA All-Star Game. A self-confessed golf junkie, Jordan couldn't pass up the chance to play at Arnold Palmer's Bay Hill Lodge. MJ didn't just come to play golf; he came to play marathon golf—54 holes in one day. Before leaving Bay Hill, he tried to set up a golf game with Arnold Palmer. It had to be on a different day, however, as he went directly from the golf course to the All-Star Game at Orlando Arena, where he scored 18 points in a 153-113 loss to the Western All-Stars. He might have overdone it with the golf that day!

You may not have the time or patience to play all 54 holes at Breezy Point in one day but, if you're here on an extended stay, I recommend you sample each of the courses during your stay. The Traditional is a shorter par-68 golf course that will test your accuracy with very tight, tree-lined fairways on many of the holes. In addition, the course features old-fashioned pushup greens that will test your chipping skills if you miss the green on your approach. Whitebirch is a longer, more open course that gives you a chance to hit your driver off the tee. They're currently putting in some new tee boxes and making other changes that will improve play there. A new turf management program has been started, which will improve the condition of the course significantly. Holes 15-17 offer a three-hole stretch with great views. Deacon's Lodge GC is consistently ranked as one of the ten best courses in the state. Arnie put the par-three 17th hole on his list of the best 18 holes ever created by the Palmer Design Company. The Golf Channel ranks this course as the third-best Arnold Palmer course the public can play. It's a "bucket list" course. You do not want to miss playing there!

Marcus, Isaiah, and Rich Aulie on Hole Number 9 at the Traditional GC. The last hole of their 54-hole marathon played on all three courses at Breezy Point- August 18, 2020.

The Ryder Cup

"Sam Ryder donated the trophy. But the inspiration and impetus which shaped the Ryder Cup's tradition of sportsmanship and friendship were provided by a local boy from Rochester. The Ryder Cup is truly Walter Hagen's baby." –author Peter Dobereiner

Walter Hagen visited Breezy Point in 1925 for the first time, playing one of the thousands of one-day exhibition matches he was famous for. In 1926, Hagen played a 72-hole winner-take-all match against England's Abe Mitchell at Royal St. George before that year's British Open.

Four down after 36 holes, Hagen rallied to win the match 2 & 1. This match was followed by an informal U.S. versus Great Britain team match won by the British side 13 ½ to 1 ½.

Despite the one-sided result, the golfers enjoyed the competition so much that it was decided to repeat it again the next year on American soil.

Sam Ryder donated a cup and paid for the British golfers' travel when the first official Ryder Cup was held in Worcester, Massachusetts, in 1927.

Teams of eight players played four partner matches on the first day and eight singles matches on the second day, with the U.S. coming out on top by a score of 9 ½ to 2 ½. It was decided to continue the matches every other year, alternating between Great Britain and the United States. Walter Hagen would captain the U.S. side for the next six matches, including the first American victory in Great Britain in 1937.

1937 was Hagen's last appearance at the Ryder Cup. The Ryder Cup has since gone on to become one of the world's top sporting events, still played in alternate years. Ryder Cup mania has found its way to the average golfer, as groups of players now mix in a Ryder Cup format when planning golf vacations with family and friends.

Breezy Point sees its share of Ryder Cup competitions every season. Groups of golfers arrive at the first tee in matching outfits for a team competition that involves some combination of best ball, alternate shot, scramble, and individual match play. Sienna's John Hankinson and his three sons started the trend in the early 2000s by inviting three friends each to Deacon's for a two- or three-day competition that became known as the Hawk Cup. The baton has since been passed to a group of players who play the aptly named Palmer Cup every year in August.

The Palmer Cup

Arnold Palmer was a two-time Ryder Cup captain and made six appearances as a player. He won 22 matches, the most by any American player.

Palmer loved the Ryder Cup, and he said, "The game brings out the best in us, and the best bring out their games at the Ryder Cup."

Following Palmer's death in 2016, Deacon's Lodge members Kevin Roberg and Jeff Smith created the Palmer Cup. The inaugural Palmer Cup was held in August 2017 at Deacon's Lodge to honor the memory and legacy of Arnold Palmer.

The annual contest is a Ryder Cup format (Palmer's favorite) contested between Team Deacon and Team Arnie. The contest is about sportsmanship, integrity, camaraderie, and the desire to play the best golf possible. All are elements that clearly defined the golf persona of Arnold Palmer.

Palmer was known as the consummate ambassador for golf. He introduced golf to the masses and, with his dynamic personality, helped us fall in love with this wonderful game. The Palmer Cup is a small way to honor a man who exemplified class, character, honesty, and everything great about the game.

The Palmer Cup was a continuation of a team event played around the world on six different continents for many years in honor of Kevin Roberg's father. Twenty-seven holes are played on Friday, featuring nine-hole partner matches in various combinations of best ball, alternate shot, and scramble, followed by individual matches on Saturday.

There is also a one-day Winnie Cup for the wives played at Whitebirch GC. The Palmer Cup has its opening ceremony on Friday morning, featuring team uniforms, a tee package for the golfers, and, of course, a Friday night party with live music and possibly an appearance by rapper "Tiny K," performing his song written in honor of the Palmer Cup!

Thanks to all the groups who put on their own Ryder Cup matches at Breezy Point, Walter Hagen's baby continues to grow the game in Breezy Point.

Frozen Fairways

Winter golf at Breezy Point in 2009

While most golf courses in Minnesota are closed in the winter, Breezy Point created a winter golf course on Pelican Lake. Since the late 1970s, Breezy has groomed the frozen bay by the marina and restaurant with white pine tree-lined fairways, greens, and flag-sticks that resemble those found on a typical golf course. After the holidays, they pick up all the unsold Christmas trees and use them to line the fairways. There might be anywhere from six to nine holes laid out on the bay, depending on where the fish houses are when the course is laid out. Like the old par-three course down by the lake, all the holes are 80 yards or less in length. Golfers use regulation golf clubs and green tennis balls while playing the "Frozen Lake Course" at Breezy Point.

Minnesota winters make it hard for golfers to keep their game in shape during the long layoff. You can roll putts on a carpet, chip balls into a chair or basket, or swing a weighted club to keep your muscles in shape. If you have enough space to swing a golf club, you can set up an indoor net in your garage and hit balls into the net.

There used to be no way to measure the distance or accuracy of balls hit into a net. The invention of computerized sensors in the 1970s began to change that. By placing microphones at different points on the net, the sound of impact could be measured and a landing spot could be estimated each time a ball was hit. With advances in technology, today's golf simulators use infrared technology to track the golf ball with optical sensors, making it possible to find the exact spot where a ball will land. Using computerized ball tracking technology, it is now possible to play a full round of golf indoors with software available that allows you to choose from a variety of different courses.

Breezy Point's newest golf professional, Nolan Toft, found that more golf courses in Minnesota were finding it necessary to add golf simulators to give their golfers a chance to play and practice during the cold Minnesota winters. Breezy purchased two Uneekor QED simulators in the fall of 2021, and two more in 2024.

Using the E6 software program, golfers can play 18 holes at Pebble Beach, Pinehurst, Torrey Pines, and many other top courses around the world. Each simulator bay can host up to eight people, with food and beverage service available at the North Star Restaurant. The simulators are equipped with the Ignite teaching and coaching program to aid the golf pro when giving lessons or doing club fitting. One of the most important factors in club fitting is finding the best shaft for your clubs. Breezy club fitters use a Mizuno shaft optimizer to measure clubhead speed, tempo, kick angle, and release factor to determine the best shaft and flex for each individual golfer.

Breezy Point's new golf simulators, located at the North Star Restaurant.

Winter is no longer a "Frozen Fairway" at Breezy Point. Throughout the year, golfers will find four golf simulators at the North Star that give them an opportunity to practice, take a lesson, get fitted for new clubs, or play a round of golf on a top-100 championship golf course.

Listen closely to the sound as your golf ball flies off the clubface and onto the simulator's screen. *Whiz! Bang!* Billy Fawcett would have loved it!

Approximately four miles out of Breezy Point, our car took a right turn off County Road 4, and a half mile later, another turn led us to the sign reading *The One at Eider Pines*, Breezy Point's newest backyard golf course.

The course designer, developer, and superintendent, Dan Bzdok, and head pro and assistant superintendent Brian Stark were there to greet us.

Brian and Biz at the firepit with "The One" in the background

A long white fence led us to the clubhouse. Inside the fence were four horses—two thoroughbreds (one a relative of Triple Crown winner Seattle Slew, the other an offspring of famed jumper Trezor) and two warmbloods of German heritage—enjoying a lazy summer day. Bzdok's wife, Jana, is a dressage rider and showed us around her horse barn. After golf, the grandkids were able to feed some carrots to the horses. Also inside the fence was a driving range with distance markers in place to aid in measuring your shots.

The clubhouse is equipped with a bar, a large-screen TV, and a golf simulator for use when the course shuts down in the winter. After a few chips and putts, we loaded our clubs on a gator and drove down to the first tee. No beverage cart today, but a bar was set up at the firepit and grilling station behind the tee. I ordered a Diet Coke while the rest of the adults enjoyed Bloody Marys.

Walking his 75-acre property six years ago, Dan discovered the flat spot we were standing on and looked at the hillside 190 yards across a large wetland area. That was the beginning of his vision to build a golf hole. A baseball and softball player, Bzdok found golf later in life and started playing seriously around age 35. A math teacher at Forestview Middle School in Brainerd, Dan worked a few summers at Eagles Landing Golf Course and later was a player assistant at the Pines at Grandview.

The idea to create a golf hole germinated in Bzdok's head for a few years until COVID-19 turned education into distance learning. After sitting at a computer teaching all day, Dan and his friend Brian needed to get away from their desks and get some exercise. Using Dan's tractor and gator, along with some hand snippers, they spent a couple hours almost every day clearing the space for the golf hole. They purchased hitting mats and mulch for the tee boxes but found everything else they needed—sand, rocks, gravel, and railroad ties—right on the property.

When finished, the hole played as a par-three over the wetlands from five different tee boxes set at 55, 77, 113, 141, and 166 yards. The original tee at 190 yards was later made into a firepit. It has a look similar to the 17th hole at Deacon's Lodge Golf Course, without elevated tee boxes. Like Deacon's 17th, the shorter tees give you a better angle to the green and make the hole play easier. One of the bunkers by the green is a bulkhead bunker framed with railroad ties angled slightly to allow for a recovery shot. It's a Pete Dye feature discovered on a trip to Scotland in 1963 where Dye saw the "sleepers" at Prestwick Golf Course. It's a nice addition and brings a Scottish touch to "The One." The sand in the bunkers is from the property and is as good as any sand you'll find on a golf course.

The One from the back tee: 166 yards

When asked how many holes in one have been made thus far, Dan replied, "None. There's no cup on the green, just a stake in the ground. We have had a couple leaners that might have qualified if there was a cup there."

Here's hoping they get a cup. I can envision a wall of fame by the firepit that records the name of everyone who makes an ace on "The One."

And finally, there's the course's name: The One at Eider Pines. Dan and Jana had a favorite dog named Eider who passed away a few years ago. Eider was buried by the sandpit just east of the first tee where some pine trees are now growing, hence the name Eider

Pines. Dan was not tempted to make The One a "dogleg" hole, but I did notice a spot across the wetlands that would make a nice dogleg-right par-four similar to the famous Cape Hole. Who knows the visions that might still exist in a golfer's mind?

Is Dan Bzdok checking out a dogleg right on the other side of the wetlands?

Chapter 11: By the Numbers

Numbers did not play a significant part in the early history of golf. Early golf clubs with their hickory shafts had names on them, not numbers. A golfer might tee off with a brassie, hit their next shot with a spoon or mashie, and play onto the green with a niblick. When the steel shaft began to replace hickory in the 1930s, matched and numbered sets of golf clubs became the norm. Now golfers used a 1- or 3-wood off the tee, hit a 3- or 5-iron next, and approached the green with their 9-iron.

Early scoring did not require numbers either. In the late 1800s, the term bogey was used to determine the score a skilled golfer might expect to make on a particular hole. At that time, scores were much higher than they are today. By the 1920s, with improvements in golf equipment and more professionals playing the game, scores began to drop.

The term par, taken from Wall Street's word for a stock's normal or "par" figure, was used as the score an expert golfer would expect to make on a hole. Par was given a number now where a short hole was considered a par-3, a medium distance hole a par-4, and the longer holes par-5.

Bogey now referred to a 1-over-par score. The expert golfer would occasionally play a hole in less-than-par figures. From the American slang term "bird," meaning anything excellent, birdie was now used to describe a score of 1-under-par on a hole. The bird theme was extended to include a score of two under par (eagle), three under par (albatross), and the near-impossible four-under-par score on a hole known as a condor.

Today, golfers are obsessed with numbers, using launch monitors in practice to measure their swing speed, smash factor, launch angle, and much more for each shot.

While playing, they might use a rangefinder to give them yardage to the pin and keep track of drives, approach shots, and putts using a program like Mark Broadie's Strokes Gained to analyze individual strokes by distance down to fractions of a stroke.

Breezy Point golfers have seen their share of numbers over the last 100 years. This chapter looks at some of the interesting numbers and the stories behind them.

The Eagle Has Landed

The golfer's equivalent of a trip to the promised land is that one swing that carries the ball directly from the tee to its ultimate destination.

"Where did my ball go?" I shouted to my youngest son as he ran down the fairway on the third hole at Cuyuna C.C. in search of his ball.

It was a late summer day in July 1991, and we were out after supper for a "fun four" holes at our local golf course.

Looking up, he asked, "Is it in the hole?"

"I don't know," I shouted back. "Let's go take a look."

After a perfect punch-draw 7-iron, I had already seen the ball go in the hole. I needed him to verify it, as he was my only witness that day.

We were the only golfers still on the course. Sure enough, when we reached the green, we found my Pinnacle Gold 2 at the bottom of the cup. A hole in one! By coincidence, I had made an ace on that hole a year earlier using a Pinnacle Gold 1 ball for my very first hole in one.

Most golfers might play their whole life without ever making a hole in one. Obviously, the more often you play and the better you are as a golfer, the more the odds will tend to swing in your favor. The average golfer is given a 12,500-to-one chance of making an ace. A low-handicap golfer's odds are 5,000 to one, and a tour pro's odds of reaching the promised land drop to 3,000 to one.

In 1939, two golfers in Indiana got into an argument after an amateur who had made a hole-in-one claimed it was easy, while a pro who had not made an ace disagreed, insisting it was a matter of math and science. He figured the odds were about 6,000 to one that it might happen in just one swing.

Bloomington, Indiana, pro Ken Welty, who became head pro at Breezy Point in 1964, wanted to test those odds. Welty decided to hit 100 shots a day for sixty days on a 135-yard par-three to see how long it would take him to make a hole in one.

The first two days, his best effort finished two inches away. On day three, he had two shots rim the cup, but still no ace. Finally, on day four, his 380th attempt landed 12 feet from the pin and trickled in. It would not count as an official ace because it didn't occur during an official round of golf and was not a one-time occurrence.

I remember making my ace late one afternoon in 1991 and hurrying to finish nine holes so it would count as an official hole in one.

Ken Welty took 600 more swings over the next six days on the 135-yard hole but didn't make another hole in one. The National Hole in One Registry gives us a statistical look at the rarity of a hole in one:

- 450 million rounds of golf are played each year.
- A hole in one is scored once in every 3,500 rounds.
- Over 128,000 holes in one are scored each year.
- One to two percent of all golfers will make a hole in one each year.
- Nine percent of golfers who make a hole in one will make three or more.
- The most holes in one: Norman Manley, with 59.
- The youngest hole in one: Jake Paine, Rancho Santa Margarita, California, three years old.
- The oldest hole in one: Harold Stilson, Boca Raton, Florida, 101 years old.
- The longest hole in one: Mike Crean, Denver, Colorado, 517 yards.
- A hole in one on a par-five is called a Condor.
- A hole in one on a par-four is called an Albatross.
- Forty percent of all holes in one are made with a 7, 8, or 9-iron.

Captain Roscoe Fawcett made a hole in one on the 136-yard fourth hole at Chippewa Links GC (Breezy's Traditional Course) on Monday, August 18, 1925. Gene Nelson and Breezy Point professional Fred Barber witnessed the shot. It is believed to be the first hole in one ever made in the Brainerd Lakes area. The original fourth hole at the Breezy Point golf course is no longer in play. After playing what is now holes 10, 17, and 18 as their first three holes, golfers would walk to the north side of the clubhouse and play from the top of the hill down toward Pelican Lake.

This picture shows Breezy professional Red Ledding and his wife, Earnie, playing the hole in the late 1950s. The course routing had been changed so Red and Earnie were playing what was then the seventh hole. Breezy Point starter Frank Cronin created a wooden plaque displayed in the clubhouse in honor of Fawcett's first ace on the hole. You will see several other plaques in the clubhouse created by Frank that commemorate other holes in one made over the years. As Rod Stewart said, "Every Picture Tells a Story," and so it is with the many holes in one made on this hole over the years.

During the 1938 Ten Thousand Lakes Tournament, eventual champion Bobby Campbell made three deuces on the par-three and never once won the hole. Two of Bobby's opponents made matching birdies, and Dick Leuthold tossed in an ace to win the hole against Campbell's birdie.

"You'll never reach it with a 7-iron, it's a 6-iron shot," said Dave Chatfield on the last day of July in 1936 as Stanton Aby, his opponent, prepared to drive on the fourth hole at Breezy Point. After a five-minute argument on the relative merits of the irons for the 136-yard hole, Aby stepped up with his preferred seven and scored an ace!

Evidently, the 7-iron was the magic weapon on this hole. On June 24, 1940, Breezy Point professional Horter McVeigh gave us an object lesson on how to break a course record. McVeigh, at the time the youngest golf pro in the United States, shot a hole in one and nipped the Breezy Point mark by two strokes with a 5-under-par 31 on the nine-hole course. He aced the 136-yard seventh hole with a 7-iron into a stiff wind.

And finally, there is this story: On June 5, 1960, long-time Breezy employee Roy Johnson took up his golf clubs after a 35-year layoff. On the 136-yard seventh hole, he made a hole in one. After the round was over, Roy decided to give up golf for good!

A hole in one made on a par-4, known as an albatross, is among the rarest of golf feats. The odds of making an albatross are approximately a million to one. Amazingly, Breezy Point's three courses have seen their share of these amazing shots. In 1981, local legend Jack Bagley hooked a 3-wood up over the trees on the 330-yard dogleg left 15th hole on the Traditional course. After a fruitless search in the woods, his ball was discovered in the hole for one amazing ace. In 2001, 10-year-old Jonas Dale of Pequot Lakes made his first hole in one at Whitebirch on Hole 17—97 yards with a 5-iron. In 2009, Dale teed it up on the 305-yard par-4 12th hole at Traditional and drove his ball over the hill in front of the green. The group putting out on the green watched Dale's ball roll onto the green and into the hole for the ultimate hole in one, an albatross. Jonas also made a one on Whitebirch's fifth hole while practicing with his high school golf team in 2007, giving him a hole in one on three different holes at Breezy Point. All before the age of 18!

*Ten-year-old Jonas Dale makes a hole in one on
Whitebirch #17.*

The closing holes at Whitebirch Golf Course feature a scenic
and challenging series of holes that have seen some magic over the
years. In 1993, Claudia DuBord scored golf's rarest bird with a
double eagle on the par-5 15th hole using her driver and a 3-wood.
Fifteen is the course's most unique hole, an up-and-down, heavily
wooded test. The last 175 yards are straight uphill to an elevated,
severely sloping green. In July of 1994, Ted Johnson, a 14-handicap

golfer, rocked his drive across the swamp on the 323-yard par-4 16th hole but didn't see it land. After searching the edge of the swamp in vain, someone suggested looking in the cup. There it was: The longest ace in Whitebirch history, an albatross on one of the golf course's signature holes.

Not to be outdone, Arnold Palmer's Deacon's Lodge course has also seen its share of albatrosses. Three days after Arnold Palmer officially opened the course, Crosslake banker Bart Taylor stepped to the tee on the 330-yard seventh hole, smashed his ball over the large wetland area and onto the green, and watched his ball roll into the hole.

It was the first hole in one at the new Palmer-designed course and the first albatross, as well. But not the last. In a one-year span between August 2010 and August 2011, Jon Sigurdson of Calgary and Ryan Ratfield of Arden Hills both aced the 329-yard 10th hole, and Jon Vanthull of Albertville holed out his tee shot on the 290-yard 8th hole. Twelve years later, Josh French of Woodbury scored an ace on the 320-yard 12th hole. Remember, the odds of making just one of those shots is a million to one!

And then we have this story, as recorded by the *Brainerd Dispatch* on July 23, 1946:

Hank Graff, local sportsman, made an ace at the Breezy Point course on Sunday afternoon . . . only it was the wrong hole. Hank teed off on number nine to finish his game. The ball, climbing over 200 feet, came down in the number eight cup just 75 feet away . . . You'll never hear the last of that, Hank!

Arnold Palmer's 21 aces range in distance from 122 to 245 yards for a total of 3,305 yards, or about 1.8 miles of unbroken magic. In 1986, during the Chrysler Cup at TPC Avenal in Maryland, Palmer aced the 182-yard third hole on consecutive days. The *Washington Post*'s Tom Boswell wrote, "On Tuesday, Arnold Palmer made a hole in one. Yesterday, he returned and made a hole in a million!"

Professional John Howard once made two consecutive holes in one at the Martini Tournament in Norwich, England, in 1971 on the par-3 11th hole and the par-4 12th hole. The odds of that ever happening are 50 million to one! I have never made consecutive aces, but in 2001, I did achieve back-to-back eagles at Whitetail Run G.C. in Wadena: a hole-in-one on the par-3 14th hole and an eagle-3 on the par-5 15th hole. I'm not sure what the odds are of that happening. Once in a lifetime for me, I'm sure!

Walter Hagen only made two holes in one in his distinguished career, but they are both great stories. In 1925, the Haig was playing a practice round for the U.S. Open Championship. He had cut his ball on the previous hole and had to borrow a new ball from playing partner Bobby Jones as he played the 180-yard sixth hole at Worcester C.C. in Massachusetts.

Walter was trying to straighten out the hickory shaft on his 2-iron when it broke over his knee, putting the club out of commission. He took his 1-iron, opened the face a bit, and hit a perfect shot that faded over a hill and into the hole.

Surely it was just a coincidence that the shot was: Hagen's first hole in one; the first time that golf ball had ever been hit; the first time anyone had ever made a one on that hole; made with a number-1-iron; and made on the first of July.

Sir Walter's second and last hole in one occurred in Oregon later that same year. It was a topped 5-iron that rolled along the ground all the way to the cup. Sometimes with a hole in one it's better to be lucky than good!

Patty Berg's hole in one on the 170-yard seventh hole at Churchill Valley C.C. during the 1959 Women's Open made her the first woman to record an ace in a USGA competition. In the summer of 1991, she recorded a hole in one at the age of 73!

Deacon's Lodge professional Mark Neva has kept a detailed record of every hole in one made at the golf course since it opened in 1999. Mark estimates the total hole-in-one distance as of 2023 is 25,599 yards, or 14.5 miles.

Visitors will find all the names and details posted on the pro shop wall leading into Palmer's Grill. It is interesting to note that the very first ace at Deacon's came on the 330-yard seventh hole, a par-4 that is the number-one handicap hole on the course!

Golfers at Deacon's have the option to purchase a beautiful plaque commemorating their ace with the Palmer logo, a drawing of the hole, and all the pertinent information engraved on it.

It's a great keepsake for those lucky enough to have made a hole in one at Arnie's course!

Notes of interest on holes in one made at Deacon's Lodge over the years:

Steve Hollinbeck is the only person with aces on two different holes—numbers three and 17—almost exactly a year apart: May 24, 2007, and May 27, 2008. Paul Willette is the only person with two aces on the same hole: number six. Willette's holes in one were made two weeks apart in May and June of 2020. Paul, Charlie, and Dylan Willette, along with Steve and Charlie Hollinbeck, are the only father-son pairs to achieve holes in one at Deacon's. Charlie Hollinbeck's ace on number six came 12 years after his dad's last hole in one. Dylan's shot on hole three, on the other hand, occurred a year before his dad made back-to-back aces, while brother Charlie joined the group near the end of the 2023 golf season with an ace on his dad's hole.

Through the 2023 golf season, golfers from 19 states and two countries have made 188 holes in one at Deacon's. Of the four par-3's, hole six has the most with 75, while hole 11 has the fewest with 19.

64 Squared

When he was a youngster, Greg Johnson's family would spend their summers at Breezy Point. While his dad drove to Brainerd to work during the day, Johnson got his start in golf going around and around Breezy Point's par-3 course down by the lake. He played high school golf at Brainerd and, after graduating, played junior college golf for Central Lakes Community College, where he qualified for the national junior college tournament. After college, he moved to California and worked on his golf game at Dad

Miller Golf Course in Anaheim, the same course Tiger Woods would play during his high school years. It is now the site of the Tiger Woods Teaching Center for underprivileged kids, as well as a premier municipal golf course in the Los Angeles area.

During the 1980s, Johnson was a fixture at the Brainerd Country Club and Breezy Point Resort. Mark Johnson recalls playing some big-money matches with him at Brainerd. He also played in most of the Breezy Point tournaments held during that time. Greg won Orv's Invitational three times in 1986, 1989, and 1995, and he holds the tournament record with a 2-over-par 212 for 54 holes in 1995. Between 1984 and 1986, the team of Johnson, Steve Stoxen, and Tim Dullum won Charlie's Scramble six months in a row. One of those wins was a 10-under-par 26, which is still the record for the lowest score at a Charlie's Scramble. Just to prove it wasn't an accident, Johnson teamed up with Breezy pro Mark Johnson and Scott Kleberg to shoot another 10-under round a few years later.

Greg turned pro in 1992 and worked as an assistant to Jim McElhaney at Breezy Point for a couple of years, helping Jim run the U.S. Golf Schools at the resort. After a summer working as an assistant at Maddens in 1994, McElhaney convinced Johnson to take a shot at the Dakotas Mini Tour to assess the state of his game. It was a good starting point for aspiring professionals, as it featured a group of professional golfers playing for good purses with reasonable entry fees. The Dakotas Tour didn't work out for Johnson, but he remains very appreciative to McElhaney for the advice and encouragement he's given him along the way. Greg also remembers a few trick shots he learned from McElhaney, including one where you first step on a golf ball, then hit down on it; as the ball pops up in the air, you hold out your golf cap and catch it! They continue to stay in touch.

In 2017, Johnson made his sixth career hole in one while playing with McElhaney's son, Jim Jr., in Nevada. He currently works at the Pines G.C. at Grandview and winters in Nevada, where he can be found playing with Champions tour players John Jacobs, Lon Hinkle, and other friends.

When I asked Greg about his course record 64, he began telling me about a 64 he shot at the Traditional golf course during their two-man tournament in 1999. When I told him I was asking about a different 64 shot at the Whitebirch golf course, he gave me a puzzled look. I was worried he might not remember the round. After handing him a blank scorecard, he studied the holes and slowly began filling in the blanks. Nine birdies, eight pars, and one bogey. Writing down a bogey four on Hole 17, Johnson looked at me with a smile and said, "I don't think I've ever played a round of golf without making at least one bogey."

The scores added up to matching totals of 32 on the front and 32 on the back for an eight-under-par 64 from the back tees at Whitebirch. Shot in the summer of 2003, it is the lowest score on record from the championship tees according to PGA Director of Golf Mark Johnson.

Amazingly, the man who learned the game as a youngster on the old par-3 course has shot 64 on two different courses at Breezy Point. If he would also shoot a 64 at Deacon's Lodge...now that would be a story. Approaching his sixth decade, Greg can still hit the ball 300 yards with his SIM2 driver and is a good putter on fast greens, using the stroke professional Joe Sodd taught him back in the 1980s at the Brainerd Country Club. No claw grip or anchored putter for this guy. If it ain't broke, don't fix it!

Johnson currently plays to a six handicap and has a goal to get it down to a two by the end of the year. Here's hoping he can make it over to Deacon's a few more times and take a shot at another 64. Then I could change the title of this story to *64 Cubed*!

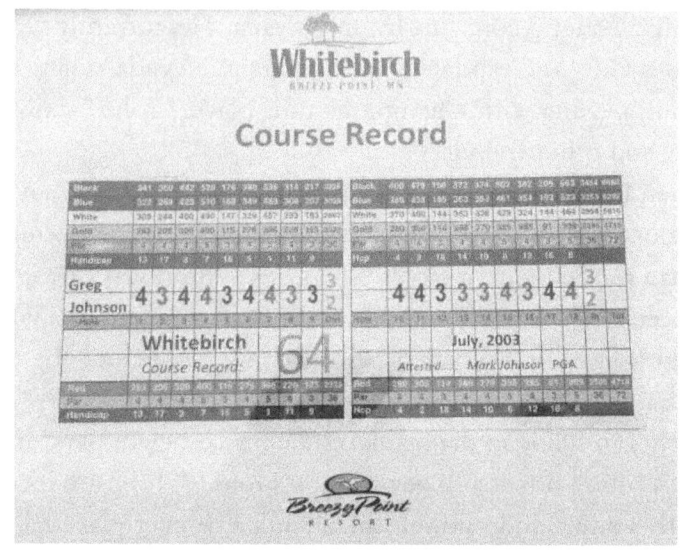

Orv Hagen, who was known to have bet a trifecta from time to time, is probably up in Heaven laying the odds on it happening right now. Those who know Greg Johnson are shaking their heads and saying, "Don't bet against it!"

Don and Greg Johnson: Two-Man Champions at Breezy Point in 1999

Mr. 62

Deacon's Lodge was designed with careful attention to players of all skill levels. The goal was to be particularly challenging from the back tees while creating a golf course that plays easier than it looks. Five or six tees on each hole are set up to give both shorter carries and easier approach angles as the player moves to the forward tees. Each level of golfer will experience a different-looking hole, as well. Like the black diamond runs at a ski slope, the black (or "King") tees at Deacon's are recommended for highly skilled golfers only.

In my first year at Deacon's, I played golf from the blue (or "Palmer") tees set at approximately 6,500 yards. My goal was to shoot even-par from the blue tees before I attempted the back tees. Late one afternoon, I holed out in the dark with a wedge on Hole 18 for an eagle three, which gave me an 18-hole score of even par-72. The next time I played, I was on the back tees, looking at a completely different golf course. Adding my score up after nine holes, I discovered I had shot 48! That was enough for me. I moved back to the blue tees.

Jesse Nelson started working at Deacon's Lodge when he was a junior in high school, loading bags and cleaning clubs and golf carts. He was a good athlete who lettered in basketball and baseball at Pequot Lakes High School. Working at Deacon's gave Jesse a chance to give golf a try. Getting by on his natural athletic ability, he was able to shoot in the mid- to high-80s on a good day.

In his second year at Deacon's, a tip from head pro Mark Neva changed Nelson's game dramatically. Mark noticed Jesse was using a baseball grip with his hands separated on the handle of the golf club. He switched him over to the interlocking grip used by Jack Nicklaus and Tiger Woods. With his hands connected, Nelson

275

became more consistent and accurate and started to break 80 regularly. He became one of the better players in the area and went on to play college golf at Bemidji State University.

It didn't hurt that most of the young men working at Deacon's played a lot of golf. Jesse estimates he may have played close to 500 rounds of golf at Deacon's Lodge in the years he worked there. Like any other skill, the more you use it, the better you get. Nelson worked outside service at Deacon's from 2003 to 2009 before turning professional and working as the assistant pro at Deacon's from 2010 to 2012. Jesse then became an assistant pro at the Pines at Grandview Lodge and earned his Class-A PGA status in 2018. He plays a good schedule of events around the state each year.

In 2019, he competed in the state PGA championship at the Preserve and won a sudden-death playoff to qualify for one of the spots in the national PGA Club Pro Championship. Unfortunately, COVID shut everything down and the national tournament was canceled, so Jesse missed out on a chance to compete on the national stage. He came back and qualified with a sixth-place finish at the 2021 state PGA held at Stonebrooke Golf Course and competed in the 2022 national tournament.

On August 29, 2012, Jesse was playing in a Pro-Member tournament at Deacon's Lodge. Playing at 6,100 yards from the white (or "Deacon") tees, he shot a 3-under-par 69. There was enough daylight left to play some more golf, so Nelson and fellow pro Greg Snow went back out to play. Moving back to the 7,000-yard black tees for this round, Jesse birdied his first four holes, sinking long putts on the third and fourth greens. Keeping his hot streak going, he added birdies at six and eight and had a three-foot birdie putt on nine to shoot 29. He missed the putt, finishing with a 6-under-par 30. It was getting late, but there was no thought of stopping.

Mark Neva had joined the twosome on the fourth hole. "After nine holes," he told me, "we knew we were watching something special. We had to pick up the pace, as the sun was beginning to go down."

Jesse missed the green on ten but chipped in for birdie. Another short birdie putt was missed on twelve, but Nelson came back to sink his birdie putt on 14 to go 8-under-par!

Earlier that year, Alexandria pro Brett Swedberg had shot an 8-under-par 64 at Deacon's. It was the lowest score anyone had posted from the back tees since the course opened in 1999. One more birdie to break the record.

Jesse's approach on Hole 16 from 140 yards out was well-struck, but it was getting too dark to see the ball land. Not finding his ball on the green, the three golfers unsuccessfully searched the area around the green. Nelson went to tend the pin while the other two putted and noticed a ball mark 10 feet short of the pin. As he reached for the flag, he saw his ball in the hole. Eagle two. Ten under par!

The only question now was: Could they finish the round in the growing darkness? Neva and Snow stopped playing and drove their cart ahead to listen for and spot Nelson's ball. Playing by sound and by feel, Jesse got up and down for par on 17 and cozied his birdie putt on 18 next to the hole for a tap in par and a course-record 62. Nine pars, eight birdies, and an eagle. Thirteen years later, the record still stands.

Jesse might have another Deacon's record with his ringer score. A ringer score is the best score ever made on each hole of the course. In twenty-some years of play at Deacon's, I have made seven eagles and 11 birdies for a ringer score of 47. Nelson has 10 eagles and eight birdies on his card for a ringer score of 44! That will be hard to beat.

In more than 2,000 exhibition matches around the country, Walter Hagen set many course records. Most of them have since been broken, but his 64 at Everett G.C. in Eagle River, Wisconsin, still stands. It is Hagen's lowest score on record. Patty Berg shot a 64 at Richmond G.C. in 1952. It was the lowest score ever recorded by any woman up to that time. Arnold Palmer shot 62 twice on the PGA Tour, but his lowest score was a course record 60 he shot at his home course, Latrobe Country Club, in 1969: 12-under-par with two bogeys! Oakmont's head professional Bob Ford had a shot at beating the record while playing in an event there in 1999 but, in deference to Mr. Palmer, picked up his ball and didn't finish his round. Hagen 64, Berg 64, Palmer 60, and Jesse Nelson 62. The best to have ever played at Breezy Point. That's pretty good company you're keeping, my friend!

Golf's Magic Number: 59

Thirty players, including Arnold Palmer's grandson Sam Saunders, have shot 59 or better in a tournament on one of the major golf tours. Al Geiberger, AKA "Mr. 59," was the first to do it in 1977. He won the 72-hole Memphis Classic without shooting a round in the 60s, scoring 72-59-72-70 to win the tournament by three shots. Jim Furyk is the only golfer with two sub-60 rounds, shooting 59 in 2013 and 58 three years later in 2016. Furyk is the only golfer to date with a 58 on one of the major tours. However, neither can claim the lowest 18-hole tournament score ever recorded. Davidson University golfer Alex Ross shot a 57 in the 2019 Dogwood Invitational in Atlanta, Georgia. Sorry, Alex—close, but no cigar. Fifty-seven years earlier, on August 19, 1962, Homero Blancas shot a 15-under-par 55 at the Premier Invitational in Longview, Texas. Sixty years later, it remains the lowest score in the history of golf.

A young hotshot golfer with an amazing short game, Blancas played for the perennial national champion University of Houston golf team. He would go on to win four times on the PGA Tour and competed on the U.S. Ryder Cup team in 1973.

The Premier Golf Course was very tight with water, out-of-bounds, and tiny domed greens providing the challenge for a golfer. After shooting 61 in the morning, Homero hit 16 of 18 greens in regulation and used only 20 putts to shoot his 55 in the afternoon round to win the tournament. He missed two putts under six feet, otherwise the round could have been even lower!

In 100 years, Breezy Point has seen its share of low rounds. In the quarterfinals of the Ten Thousand Lakes Tournament in 1957, both John Biernet and Rolf Deming shot 66.

Biernet made a birdie on the first playoff hole to win their match 1-up. In the 1971 Billy Fawcett finals, Doug Nelson was 5-under-par with seven threes in the 11 holes it took to defeat Don Heidt 7 & 5. Three-time Breezy Invitational champion Greg Johnson shot 64 in a best-ball tournament in 1999, and two-time Invitational champion Peter Hoffman remembers shooting 65, 64, 64, and 61 at the Traditional one week in 1987. He couldn't get a match with anyone for the rest of that summer! These are just some of the great rounds at the Traditional course over the years, but not close to the record. In August of 1967, club champion Don Heidt made his way around the Traditional course in golf's magic number, shooting a 59!

Heidt was a long hitter. Peter Birkeland played a lot of golf with Don and remembers him being able to drive his ball over the green on Hole Number 1. Greg Johnson recalls Heidt telling him that the trees on the Breezy course weren't very tall in 1967, allowing Don to shoot over them and cut the distance down on many of the holes. With his length, many of the holes were just a pitch and a putt. And, when his putter was hot, Heidt could make a lot of birdies.

Don learned to play golf while working as a frontman for Oral Roberts in the 1950s. With all the events being held at night, there was time off during the day, and golf became a way to pass the time in between revivals. A single-digit handicapper, Heidt came to Breezy Point in 1963 and was involved in the construction around the resort, including a new golf clubhouse built by his company. Don lived in a Swiss A-frame by the eighth hole and would use his golf cart to play as many holes as he could after work each day, often using only his 7-iron, wedge, and putter, occasionally pausing to dedicate the shot he was hitting to another player or friend. He was the Breezy Point club champion and won the Billy

Fawcett Tournament in 1969 and 1973. Heidt was a fixture in the local golf scene from the 1960s through the 1980s, along with his frequent golfing companion, Father Edward Rahmacher.

Don Heidt holding the 1969 Billy Fawcett Memorial trophy with runner-up Mike Spielmann on his right and Mike's dad, Harold, on his left

How Low Can You Go? Vision54 Comes To Breezy Point

In his quest for perfection, famed golfer Ben Hogan would play golf in his sleep. One night, he dreamed that he made 17 straight holes in one. In his bid for 18 in a row, the ball lipped out of the cup. Hogan recalled that he was "madder than hell" when that happened!

Lynn Marriott and Pia Nilsson created their Vision54 golf school to help golfers shoot lower scores. Marriott and Nilsson are the two highest-ranked female instructors in the country. They have coached ten different major winners and four number-one ranked players in the world, including the only woman to shoot 59 in an LPGA tournament round, Annika Sorenstam. Their Vision54 school has been ranked the best golf school in America. It's based on their belief that it's possible to shoot 54 or lower for 18 holes. Vision54 targets the whole person, not just the technical side of the game.

Rob Birkeland had attended a Vision54 school in Iowa with his friend Rich Reese. Rich's daughter Kristine was an instructor with the Vision54 program. They thought it would be fun to bring the school to Breezy Point so, in the summer of 2006, Vision54 came to Deacon's Lodge for a week.

Lynn and Pia moved their golfers from the practice tee to the putting green, then to the clubhouse for classroom work, and out onto the golf course, where they practiced not just the technical side of golf, but also the physical, emotional, mental, social, and spiritual aspects of the game. At the end of the week, anyone working at the golf course could take part in a half-day Vision54 class. I jumped at the chance to learn a little bit about their program.

We all got a great lesson in how to get out of our own way so we could play *golf* instead of playing *golf swing* all the time. It was very liberating and made a marked improvement in my game.

Breezy Point has seen its share of low rounds throughout the years. With the latest advances in equipment, as well as young golfers becoming bigger, stronger, and faster, and programs like Vision54 pushing mental barriers, it will be interesting to see how low golfers might go at Breezy Point's golf courses in the future.

One Minute and 39.2 Seconds

Rick Aulie didn't participate in many team sports when he was in high school. He was a Golden Gloves boxer in the winter, ran cross-country in the fall to get in shape for boxing, and played golf in the spring. He was a good athlete, a state champion, and a two-time Upper Midwest finalist in boxing. He also qualified for state in cross country in his junior and senior years and was a five-time all-conference winner in golf.

After graduating from college, his new passion became running marathons. He qualified for the Boston Marathon in 2019 and finished near the top in his age division.

In January 2018, Aulie watched a video of Englishman Steve Jeffs playing a 500-yard golf hole in one minute and 50.6 seconds, which at the time was recognized as the world record for the fastest hole in golf. "I looked at it and thought, 'I could do that,'" he said. "I love to run. I love to play golf. I love a challenge. Put those three things together, and here we go."

To be considered for the record, a golfer must finish a hole with the same number of clubs with which they started, and the hole must be more than 500 yards. Timing begins the moment of the first stroke and ends when the ball settles in the hole. A member at Breezy Point's Whitebirch Golf Course, "Slick Rick" chose the 503-yard par-5 fourth hole at Whitebirch as the site of his world record attempt. The date he chose for his attempt at the record was July 26, in honor of his 34th birthday. Win, lose, or draw, there was going to be a party afterward!

Family and friends were on hand to watch his try at the record that day, along with representatives from Breezy Point and a local newspaper. The *Brainerd Dispatch* photographer had a drone with a video camera attached, which would follow him every step of the way. Rick brought his driver, 3-wood, wedge, and putter along to use on the par-5 hole. The rules would require him to carry all four clubs with him as he played the hole.

His first drive went a little bit right, and the stopwatch began timing him. Running to the ball, he dropped his bag, took out the 3-wood, and struck his second shot. The ball hit a tree and veered off to the left. He was not able to recover from that, resulting in a time that was too slow.

Back to the tee for attempt number two, this time Aulie pushed his drive even farther right. Arriving at his ball, he decided to abandon attempt number two. Thinking he might have enough gas left for one more attempt, he went back to the tee for a third try at the record.

This time, his drive was down the middle and long. Taking his time on the second shot, he smoothed a 3-wood up just short of the green. Racing to the ball, he used his wedge to pitch the ball close to the hole for a tap-in birdie. One minute and 39.2 seconds; a new world record! Let the party begin!

"Best birthday ever," Aulie said.

An old saying goes that records are made to be broken. Almost 11 months later to the day, on June 25, 2019, Belgian professional Thomas Detry played the 523-yard par-5 10th hole at Real Club de Golf in Spain in one minute and 29.6 seconds, setting a new record for the world's fastest golf hole. But I'm wondering if that's the actual record for the fastest hole?

The rules state that to be considered for the record, the hole must be at least 500 yards in length and timing begins the moment of the first stroke and ends when the ball settles in the hole. In 2002 at the Green Valley Ranch G.C. in Denver, Colorado, Mike Crean played the 517-yard par-5 ninth hole in one stroke!

A hole in one on a par-5 is called a condor. A condor is so

uncommon in golf that the odds of someone making a one on a par-5 is more than 90 million to one. Assuming the ball took 10 to 15 seconds to reach and eventually settle in the hole, in my opinion, that would qualify as the world's fastest hole of golf!

Though it only lasted for a brief time, the record did happen here at Breezy Point in 2018. If you happen to be playing at Whitebirch G.C. sometime when it's not too crowded, tee a ball up on Hole Number 4 and see how long it takes you to get the ball to settle in the hole. I recommend you not use your golf cart.

I tried following Rick on his fastest-hole run, and my golf cart couldn't keep up with him! If you time yourself, you might be surprised by how fast one minute and 39 seconds goes by!

Rick Aulie on the run for the fastest hole in golf world record

Finished in one minute and 39.2 seconds for a new world record!

Ten Thousand Lakes Golf Tournament Champions

Men's Champions

1924	R.C. Lilly d. Roscoe Fawcett 3 & 2
1925	Les Bolstad d. Roscoe Fawcett 4 & 3
1926	Art Tveraa d. Les Bolstad 1 up 21 holes
1927	Harry Legg d. D.N. Tallman 6 & 4
1928	Harry Legg d. Art Tveraa 2 & 1
1929	Roscoe Fawcett d. Henry Howe 4 & 3
1930	Les Bolstad d. Jake Wetherby 3 & 1
1931	Rudy Juran d. N.E. Swanson 5 & 3
1932	Les Bolstad d. Conway Bolstad 4 & 2
1933	Les Bolstad d. John Barnum 1 up
1934	Stan Larson d. Larry Dail 6 & 5
1935	Stan Larson d. W. H. Fawcett Jr. 4 & 2
1936	Jimmy Deeble d. Ed Cox 6 & 5
1937	Maurice Cain d. Neil Croonquist 4 & 2
1938	Bobby Campbell d. Babe LeVoir 3 & 2
1939	Herman Berg Jr. d. William Sorenson 5 & 3
1940	Dean Ritchie d. Ernotte Hiller 1 up
1941	Dean Ritchie d. Jimmy Harris 4 & 3
1942-1945	World War II – No tournament
1946	Gene Wright d. F. S. Brinkman 3 & 1
1947-1954	No tournament
1955	Roy Widstrom d. Ken Young 1 up in 19
1956	Ken Young d. John Biernat 3 & 2

1957	Tom Hadley d. John Biernat 7 & 5
1958	Bill Waryan d. Ken Young 4 & 3
1959	Len Bjorklund d. Art Hays Jr. 3 & 1
1960	Len Bjorklund d. Al Lerum 6 & 5
1961	No tournament
1962	Len Bjorklund
1963	Art Hays Jr. 141 (36 holes medal play)
1964	John Taylor 175 (45 holes medal play)
1965	Kenny Pinns 69 (rain shortened)
*	In 1966, the tournament was renamed the Billy Fawcett Memorial Golf Tournament
1966	Don Peddie 147 (36 holes medal play)
1967	Art Hays Jr. d. Ding Howell 1 up
1968	No tournament
1969	Don Heidt d. Mike Spielmann 2 & 1
1970	Rich Aulie d. Don Heidt 4 & 2
1971	Doug Nelson d. Don Heidt 8 & 7
1972	Doug Nelson
1973	Don Heidt
1974	Mark Patnode
1975	R J Smiley d. Mac Alexander
1976	Dan Strimple d. R J Smiley 5 & 4
1977	Tony Gould
1978	Chuck Meyer d. Terry Sopko 2 & 1
1979	John Hoffman d. Chuck Meyer 4 & 3
1980	Joe Towle d. John Hoffman 1 up
1981	Mark Alexander d. Don Heidt
1982	Jerry Whelan
1983	Tony Palaia d. Scott Grams 5 & 4
1984	Vic Villella d. Todd Anderson

1985	Jerry Whelan d. Terry Sopko 2 & 1
1986	Chuck Meyer d. Dick Pobuda 3 & 2
1987	Rich Villela d. Terry Sopko 4 & 2
1996	Greg Johnson d. Mitch Knutson
2001	Terry Norblom d. John Vanstrom 2 up

Women's Champions

1924	Mrs. Ralph Little d. Mrs. Roscoe Fawcett 5 & 4
1925	Mrs. Ralph Little d. Mrs. Edward C. Anderson
1926	Mrs. Ralph Little d. Mrs. Wm Freeman 2 & 1
1927	Mrs. Orren Safford d. Mrs. Little in 21 holes
1928	Mrs. Orren Safford d. Mrs. Roscoe Fawcett 5 & 4
1929	Mrs. Ralph Little d. Mrs. Sam Waters 4 & 2
1930	Mrs. Ralph Little d. Donna Lycan 4 & 3
1931	Mrs. Roscoe Fawcett d. Betty Hays 4 & 3
1932	Mrs. Ralph Little d. Mrs. Roy Quigley 4 & 3
1933	Patty Berg d. Betty Hays 2 & 1
1934	Patty Berg d. Dorothy Lanpher 3 & 1
1935	Patty Berg d. Mrs. A. W. Clapp 7 & 5
1936	Edith Kierland d. Gertrude Anderson 1 up
1937	Ann Haroldson (medal play winner)
1938	Mrs. E.F. Cary (medal play winner)
1955	Mrs. W. A. Couch d. Mrs. Fred Everett 4 & 3
1956	Mrs. Enid Fitzsimmons
1957	Clara Morgan d. Mrs. R.F.B. Cote 4 & 3
1958	Clara Morgan (medal play Winner)
1959	Mrs. Kathy Rawitzer d. Mrs. Jane Hastings
1965	Bev Vanstrom 40 (rain shortened)

1966	Beatsie Fieldman d. Monie Deveraux 2 & 1
1967	Beatsie Fieldman d. Julie Dinsmore 4 & 2
1976	Jean Alexander d. Fran Murphy
1977	Jean Lindell
1978	Jean Lindell
1979	Jean Lindell
1980	Jean Lindell d. Jean Alexander
1981	Jean Alexander
1982	Jean Lindell
1983	Jean Lindell d. Bev Wooley 6 & 4
1984	Pat Bartholomew d. Jean Alexander
1985	Pat Bartholomew d. Jean Lindell 2 & 1
1986	Bea Passolt d. Pat Bartholomew 3 & 2
1987	Pat Bartholomew d. Jean Lindell 1 up
1996	Vicki Austad d. Jean Lindell

Breezy Point Invitational:
"Orv's Invitational"

Year	Champion	Score	Runner-Up	Score
1980	John Hoffman		Chuck Meyer	
1981	Joe Towle			
1982	Joe Towle		Dale Severson	
1983	Joe Towle			
1984	Joe Towle	217	Steve Stoxen	223
1985	Joe Towle	220	Greg Johnson	230
1986	Greg Johnson	218	Dennis Burr, Peter Hoffman	223
1987	Tom Dvorak	216	Scott Sorum	218
1988	Scott Sorum	175	Tom Dvorak	181
1989	Greg Johnson	213	S. Sorum, P. Hoffman	216
1990	Peter Hoffman	224	Chuck Meyer	229
1991	Scott Sorum	213	Peter Hoffman	220
1992	Vic Villela			
1993	Peter Hoffman	216	Bill Bigler	223
1994	Scott Sorum	219	Vic Villela	220
1995	Greg Johnson	212	Brant Elson	214
1996	Scott Sorum	215	Peter Hoffman	215
1997	Scott Sorum	215	Bill Bigler	223

1988 tournament was shortened to 45 holes because of rain.
1995 Greg Johnson sets tournament record with a 2-over-par total of 212.
1996 Scott Sorum and Rush Creek pro Peter Hoffman tied at the end of regulation. Sorum drained an 18-foot putt for birdie on the first extra hole for the win.

Five-time champion Joe Towle (left). Five-time champion Scott Sorum and two-time winner Peter Hoffman (below, left to right).

Chapter 12: Through the Years, Breezy Point's Golf Professionals

1924 – Lincoln F. "Link" Howatt

Link Howatt started his career in golf as a caddie master at the Town and Country Club in St. Paul, was promoted to assistant pro, and took over when head pro Jack Burke left in 1921. Howatt was recognized for the rapid development shown by the beginning golfers he instructed. He also supervised construction work on the Breezy Point course before the grand opening on July 4, 1924. After leaving Breezy, he designed and built a nine-hole course in Dillon, Montana, built a second nine holes for Detroit C.C. in Detroit Lakes, Minnesota, and served as a golf professional in Utah.

1925 – Fred Barber

A Los Angeles city champion, Barber competed against Walter Hagen on his visit to Breezy Point in 1925. Barber shot 82 to Hagen's 77.

1926-1931 – Herb Crummy

Crummy learned the game as a caddie at the Minikahda Club. He spent his winters in Los Angeles teaching golf and summers as head pro at Breezy Point, where he held the course record of 71 until 1930. Herb's teaching prowess was reported in the 1931 *Golfer and Sportsman* magazine: "Until three months ago Mrs. Annette Fawcett hardly knew the difference between a driver and a putter, and certainly nothing at all about what you were supposed to do with them. Under the watchful eye of Herb Crummy, the genial young professional attached to the Breezy Point club, Mrs. Fawcett demonstrated that there is some sort of short cut to par golf."

1932 – Archie Houle

1933 – Les Madison

Les Madison was a golf professional in Arizona and California in the 1920s and 30s. He came to Breezy Point in 1933 and the next year took a position at Hollywood Golf Club. He was a very good player who qualified for the U.S. Open in 1932 and 1933. In 1933, at North Shore G.C., he finished 54th with a 312 total, 25 shots behind champion Johnny Goodman. The Lester Firm from Breezy Point (Les Bolstad and Les Madison) teamed up to dominate in the 1933 Minnesota Open at Edina C.C. They won the pre-tournament Pro-Am with a best ball 5-under-par 67. Madison then won the pro's long drive contest with a 268.5-yard average for three drives, and Bolstad went on to win his first state open with a four-round score of 292. Les Bolstad credited work on his short game, under the direction of pro Les Madison, with his fine play that year. The two would often travel together while playing the winter tour in the 1930s. The Hollywood pro was featured in a 1937 *Sports Illustrated* article where he admitted that it's not a hard job at all teaching the game to Jean Harlow and Ruby Keeler! Eventually, he went on to bigger and better things. In 1957, the *LA Times* stated that ex-pro Les Madison found gold in building up automobile agencies and selling them. He was a buffalo breeder at one time and now runs horses. His thoroughbred, Beau Madison, had just set a record of 45 seconds flat for the half-mile. Les passed away in 1999 at the age of 93.

1935 – Leon Rasmussen

1940 – Horter McVeigh (profiled in Chapter 4)

1941-1942 – Willard Kottke

1946 – Jim Pringle

A native of Scotland, Jim Pringle was an assistant to Willie Kidd at Interlachen C.C. in the 1930s. While there, he taught a young beginner named Patty Berg. A noted instructor, Jim was featured in an instruction series in the *Minneapolis Star* newspaper in 1936: "The Fundamentals of the Perfect Swing for Women Golfers." Pringle went on to serve as the head pro at Minneapolis G.C. as well as in North Dakota before coming to Breezy Point. He owned and operated a driving range in Bloomington in the 1950s.

1948 – Don MacRae

1949 – Bobby Krig

1952-1962 – Red Ledding (profiled in Chapter 5)

1963 – Max Evans (profiled in Chapter 5)

1964-65 – Ken Welty

Ken Welty had been following the golf game since he was an 11-year-old caddie back in Indiana. He turned pro in 1938, and it was in 1939 that Ken's entrepreneurial spirit was first displayed when he promoted a contest to see how many shots it would take him to make a hole in one on a par-3 at his golf course. Shades of Walter Hagen and the Mysterious Montague, he later put on an archery/golf match at his golf course. Welty played with regular golf clubs while an archer shot an arrow on each hole. Like the Haig and Monty, Ken and the archer shot matching scores for nine holes.

Always one to think outside the box, Welty was the head pro in Billings, Montana, in 1941 when he thought it might be fun if he and his friend Richard Hughes could tee it up in the Western Open in Phoenix, Arizona, the next week. It was the middle of January, and neither golfer had swung a club in over three months, but for an entry fee of $7.50, they found themselves in the tournament. It took the golfers two and a half days of hard driving to cover the 1,400 miles to Phoenix in Ken's 1938 Roadster. Unable to play a practice round, they found a driving range nearby where they could hit the bag of practice balls they brought with them. While warming up, they noticed Ben Hogan practicing on one side of them and Sam Snead hitting balls on the other side. It was a difficult adjustment going from the sand greens of Montana to the grass greens in Phoenix without any time to practice. Welty shot a first-round 90, and neither Montana golfer came close to making the cut. They were able to spend the rest of the week watching the best players in the world play. Porky Oliver won the tournament, while Hogan and Byron Nelson tied for second place. Ken worked at the Lakewood Golf Course in Wilmington, California, after World War II and ended up replacing Max Evans at Breezy Point in 1964.

Following his time at Breezy, he returned to California and could be found still giving lessons at El Segundo golf course in 1975.

1966 – Willie Mund

1971-1976 – Doug Nelson

Doug Nelson was a member of the 1966 state high school championship golf team from North Branch and played on the St. Cloud State College golf team from 1967 to 1971. He won the Billy Fawcett tournament in 1971 and 1972 while he was working at Breezy. After his time at Breezy Point, Doug spent time as an assistant pro in South Dakota and at the Denver C.C. before moving to Vail, Colorado, where he was the head pro at Singletree GC in Vail from 1978 to 1987. Following a short period at Sylvania C.C. in Toledo, Ohio, he applied for and was hired as head pro at the Minikahda Club in 1995, a position he held until retiring in 2015. Nelson was the recipient of the MN PGA Golf Professional of the Year award in 2013. Now retired and living in Bay Lake, Minnesota, Doug still enjoys returning to Breezy Point from time to time for an occasional round of golf.

1976 – Dan Strimple (profiled in Chapter 7)

1989 – Dave Williams

1992-1993 – Jim McElhaney

A Breezy Point teaching professional in 1992 and 1993, Jim McElhaney was from Breckenridge, Minnesota. Jim won the state high school golf championship in 1959, shooting 79-74 at the University Golf Course. After graduating from the University of Hawaii, he turned pro in 1966. McElhaney worked as an assistant pro at Braemar GC in Edina for two years before moving to the Fargo area. For the next twelve years, Jim worked at the Fargo C.C. and later at Oxbow Golf Course. In the early 1970s, Jim became a trick-shot golf artist, following the path of Walter Hagen's friends Joe Kirkwood and Mysterious John Montague by doing exhibitions around the country. He was a walking encyclopedia of knowledge on golf names, events, and rules. McElhaney started the week-long U.S. Golf Schools at Breezy, aided by assistants Howard Snyder and Rusty Allen in 1992, and Brainerd's Greg Johnson in 1993. Allen was a former tour player who caddied for his uncle, Tommy Bolt, for a time. Jim wintered as a teaching professional in Sedona, Arizona.

1994 – Al Johnston

A native of Glasgow, Scotland, Al Johnston competed on the PGA Tour from 1960 to 1968. Johnston won the 1962 Hot Springs Open in a sudden-death playoff with Bill Collins with a birdie on the second playoff hole. The win made Al a life member of the PGA. He was a member of Canada's 1962 World Cup team and won the 1966 Canadian Professional Match Play tournament as well. Prior to coming to Breezy Point, Johnston held club pro jobs in Florida, New York, and LaQuinta C.C. and Desert Horizons C.C. in California. Al was a partner in the Haney-Johnston Golf Academy in Palm Desert, California, and brought a positive attitude and a wealth of experience to his teaching.

1995 – Jerry Hoffman

1997-1998 – Ken Lubke

1999-present – Mark Johnson, Director of Golf

1999-present – Mark Neva, Deacon's Lodge GC

2021-present – Nolan Toft, Whitebirch and Traditional GC

2023-present – Ryan Sharpe, teaching professional.

100 Years of Golf at Breezy Point: From Hagen to Palmer

In the spring of 2020, as part of a plan to downsize our lives, my wife Mary and I sold our home on Serpent Lake in Crosby, Minnesota, and purchased a one-level home in Breezy Point on the third hole of the Traditional golf course. We moved into our new home on June 18. I remember standing in front of the large windows overlooking the golf course with a smile on my face. It wasn't because after 55 years as a golfer I finally lived on a golf course. In fact, there are three 18-hole golf courses at Breezy Point: the original Chippewa Links, now known as the Traditional, Whitebirch GC, just a driver and a wedge from where we now live, and the Arnold Palmer-designed Deacon's Lodge GC, which opened in 1999 with Palmer on hand to play the opening round on Memorial Day. I was one of the men holding the ropes around the tee that day as Palmer and Minnesota Governor Jesse Ventura hit their opening tee shots. It was my first day on the job as a Player's Assistant at Deacon's, a job I still have today.

But it wasn't all the wonderful golf courses right in my backyard that had me smiling. No, I was thinking of a day almost 50 years ago when I was walking the fairways of the Traditional GC and playing in the championship match of the Billy Fawcett Memorial Golf Tournament. The tournament had its beginnings back in

1924 when it was called the Ten Thousand Lakes Golf Tournament. It was a fixture every year around the first part of July and attracted many of the top amateur golfers in the state. Play consisted of 18 holes of qualifying followed by four rounds of match play over three days. On the corner table next to the windows sits the trophy I received after defeating defending champion, Don Heidt, in the final match in 1970. Billy Fawcett's youngest son, Roscoe, was at the awards ceremony to present me the championship trophy. Lots of great memories. They always bring a smile to my face!

I was also remembering a call I had received a month earlier from my 12-year-old grandson. Isaiah lives on the Whitebirch GC and is a member here. "Grandpa," he said, "I played at the Traditional today. I bogeyed the first hole, birdied the second, and then all heck broke loose!" I asked him what happened. "I teed off with the 3-wood you gave me and then holed out my wedge for an eagle 2!"

I congratulated him and told him that his dad had probably never done anything like that. Exactly one week later, I received a text from Isaiah's dad, Rick, telling me that he had driven the green on number three and made the putt for his own eagle. As you can see, the Aulies are a very competitive family!

It also got me thinking about how many other memories must have been created on the fairways of the Breezy Point golf courses over the past 100 years. This book gave me a chance to explore the history of golf at Breezy Point. What I found was a rich history with a focus on families. From the Fawcett family in the 1920s to the Spizzo family in the 2020s, Breezy Point has always been about bringing people together to create lasting memories. Whether you're an employee, a guest, or a resident of the town, everyone is a part of the family known as Breezy Point Resort. That's the way it was, that's the way it is today, and hopefully, that's the way it will be for another 100 years.

Rich Aulie
Breezy Point, July 22, 2024

This painting by artist Amanda Toft shows the original Breezy Point Golf Course painted over a black-and-white photo of the resort taken in 2021. Her artistic style leans toward an impressionistic approach that is textured and colorful. Her husband, Nolan, is the PGA professional at the Whitebirch and Traditional golf courses at Breezy Point.

Afterword

"Golf should be a pleasure, not a penance." –Donald Ross, Pinehurst Golf Course architect

In April of 1923, Captain Billy wrote, "Mrs. Fawcett and I took our first lessons in golf at Pinehurst, NC last winter, so that germ has been planted." Playing in a professional golf tournament at Pinehurst in the 1930s, Billy Fawcett's friend Les Bolstad wrote, "This country (Pinehurst) with its sand hills and pines and with the bunch grass for rough resembles nothing so much as Breezy Point."

Diamondhead president and Pinehurst Resort CEO Bill Maurer said in 1973: "Maybe I'm not the first to propose a Golf Hall of Fame, but I'm the first to do it." As a youngster, Breezy Point champion golfer Greg Johnson remembers summers at Breezy where he would go around and around the old Par 3 course for days at a time. "As a toddler. this course was my playpen," Johnson told me.

Land developer and golf course architect Bill Maurer created the World Golf Hall of Fame at Pinehurst in 1973. Three of the thirteen original Hall of Fame members have played golf at Breezy Point. Maurer laid out the back nine of the Traditional Golf Course at Breezy Point in 1963 and also built a nine-hole Par 3 course down by Pelican Lake that has since been abandoned. Recent word from Breezy Point indicates a Par 3 course is coming back.

In 2017, architect Gil Hanse used 10 acres of land from the old course at Pinehurst to create a Par 3 masterpiece called the Cradle—798 yards of fun in the sun with its own bar aptly named the Pinecone. Continuing the Pinehurst-Breezy connection, Breezy Point intends to take land from their original golf course and create its own Par 3 playground, replete with piped in music and lights for play at night. Noted golf course architect Andy Staples has been hired to build the par 3 course on the site of the East Traditional golf holes. Staples commented that, "We intend to make this course a tribute to the history of golf course architecture and to the Traditional Course and all who have played and cherished it over the years. I see no reason why it won't make *Golf Digest*'s list of the 12 most fun golf courses in America!"

The 12-hole short course will bring a touch of Ireland and Scotland to Minnesota with templates of some of the greatest holes in golf converted to par 3s. The 10-hole Bill Maurer design on the West Traditional side will all be enhanced and converted to a par 3 design as well. In a tribute to its past, the course's new social club will honor longtime general manager Dave Gravdahl, who passed away in 2024. There will hopefully be an area in the clubhouse to display historical moments from the past, and maybe even some bags of hickory-shafted clubs for anyone who wants to go back to the future and play like it's 1924 again! The quotes above show a longstanding connection between Pinehurst, the home of American golf, and Breezy Point. Breezy is truly the Pinehurst of Minnesota golf, and the addition of a Par 3 course will only add to that connection. Dave Gravdahl would have loved it, and if Breezy Point founder Captain Billy Fawcett were here, he would no doubt be leading the parade to the first tee with fireworks in hand.

Here's to the next 100 Years of Golf at Breezy Point!

Acknowledgments

Vince Font and Glass Spider Publishing for the work involved in editing and formatting the book to get it ready for publishing. Great service and value. For a first-time author, Glass Spider was a perfect fit.

Pete Mohs, publisher at *Lake Country Echo* and the *Brainerd Dispatch* for digging out back issues for me to peruse in my research (a veritable gold mine of information) and permission to use anything I found for the book.

Mark Neva, PGA pro at Deacon's Lodge, who always had time for a cup of coffee and a conversation about the book. Mark provided several items I was able to include in the book.

My wife, for her support and encouragement throughout the three-year journey of writing this book. Love you, Mary! I couldn't have done this without you.

To all the people who let me use the photos credited in the book, thank you!

To all the people, too many to name, who provided time over the phone or with an in-person interview. The spirit of golf at Breezy

Point is evident in the stories you shared, which helped shape the narrative of this book.

Author Curt Sampson, who was kind enough to share his thoughts on the blueprint and timeline involved in getting the words organized to tell the story of golf at Breezy Point.

My friend Brian Gaffney, who helped with and basically wrote the introduction to the book.

And finally, Breezy Point owner Bob Spizzo, who asked me in 2021 if I had any ideas for Breezy Point's upcoming centennial celebration. And so, to paraphrase the words Captain Billy Fawcett wrote back in 1923, "the germ had been planted" for *100 Years of Golf at Breezy Point*.

About the Author

Rich Aulie has been around golf most of his life, first as a player, and then as a Minnesota high school hall of fame golf coach for 37 years. Aulie first played golf at Breezy Point in 1967, won the Billy Fawcett golf tournament there in 1970, and has worked at Arnold Palmer's Deacon's Lodge Golf Course since 1999. A retired teacher, Rich and his wife, Mary, live on the third hole of Breezy Point's Traditional Golf Course, where he now only plays golf on days that end in "Y"!

Photo Credits

10, 18, 25, 37, 56–57, 83, 107, 111–112, 114–117, 120–122, 127, 132 (top), 134, 138, 164, 169, 172, 175, 178, 185–187, 195, 197, 233, 246, 249, 253, 265, 294, 295, 297 Breezy Point Resort archives

27, 52–53, 123, 137, 158, 173, 190–191, 217, 220, 228, 230–231, 245, 249, 251, 253, 255–257, 259–260, 270, 274, 278, 279, 281, 310 Rich Aulie

73, 75, 88, 90, 96, 97, 99–100, 109, 119, 151, 159, 162, 177, 182, 183, 188–189, 193, 198, 200–201, 203, 210, 223, 235, 244, 267, 270, 274, 293, 299, 300, 301 *Lake Country Echo*

82, 105, 113, 129, 134, 139, 156, 168, 170, 236–237, 282 *Brainerd Dispatch*

286-287 *Brainerd Dispatch* courtesy Steve Kohls

39, 41, 45, 49, 93–95, 97 *Amateur Golfer and Sportsman*

13, 15, 21 –Wikipedia/Wiki

65, 166 *Minneapolis Star*

58, 71 the Otis Dypwick family

48 Jeff and Mary Smith

102 the Ryan family

69 the Berg family

176 the Landecker family

205 the Chapman family

163 John Hoffman

222 Erik Larsen

215, 225 Breezy Point Resort

240 Chris Olson

305 Amanda Toft